What I Wish I Knew Years Ago

SAM BRADY

Copyright © 2025 by Sam Brady

All rights reserved. No part of this book may be reproduced by any mechanical, photographic, or electronic process, or in the form of a phonographic recording; nor may it be stored in a retrieval system, transmitted, or otherwise be copied for public or private use—other than for "fair use" as brief quotations embodied in articles and reviews-without prior written permission of the author and publisher.
The author of this book does not dispense medical advice or prescribe the use of any technique as a form of treatment for physical, emotional, or medical problems without the advice of a physician, either directly or indirectly. The intent of the author is only to offer information of a general nature to help you in your quest for emotional, physical, and spiritual wellbeing. In the event you use any of the information in this book for yourself, the author and the publisher assume no responsibility for your actions.

Book designer: Sam Brady

Book editor: Sam Brady

Published by Hindsight Publishing

Paperback ISBN: 979-8-218-87359-2

First edition, December 2025

What I wish I knew Years ago

For my Mum Diane.

Thank you for always being there for me.

Even when I'm being crazy.

CHAPTERS

INTRODUCTION   1

CHANGE   8
A New and Improved Self
It's Going to Get Ugly Before It Gets Beautiful
Beliefs - Just Because You Believe It, It Does Not Make It True
Change Is the Only Way to Transform

HEALING FROM PAST TRAUMA   25
Triggers
What Is Actually Happening to Your Brain
New Conscious Behaviour
Healing Is an Ongoing Job

GET RID OF WHAT YOU DON'T WANT   41
Get Prepared to Cut Off the Dead Wood
You'll Naturally Filter Out the Bad and Be Left with The Good
Choose What Your 'Tunnel Vision' Is On
How to Deal with Roadblocks

MINDSET AND THOUGHTS   58

Be Aware, Observe ... But Don't Hold On

Positivity and Optimism

You Can Choose How You React

You Are More Than Just the Voice in Your Head

CONFIDENCE   71

Why It's Essential

The Right Kinda Confidence

Rewind and Rewire!

New Self Assurance

LAW OF ATTRACTION   82

What It Is

How to Use It

The Art of Being Patient

Trust

MANIFEST WHAT YOU WANT   99

Goals and Dreams - Get Clear

What's Your Calling?

Receiving Can Feel Uncomfortable ...

Always Expect It!!

Grow with The Flow

LET'S GET SPIRITUAL   113

Spirituality and Your Own Energy

Reiki Healing and Chakras

Shadow Work

Benefits of - Hridaya Mudra/Crystals/Sage/Incense/Oils

MAKE IT YOUR NEW WAY OF LIFE   145

It's Your Time to Forget the Past and Create the Future That You Want

Make Plans, Not Excuses

A Three-Part Cocktail Mix of 'Surrendering. Habits. Gratitude'

There Is Only the Eternal Now

An Ongoing Masterpiece

AFTERWORD   164

INTRODUCTION

I'm here to get real with you. If you want a better life, you can have it. Just be prepared for the highs, the lows ... and most importantly, getting out of your current comfort zone. Transforming your life, growing, and evolving are all difficult, yet beautiful. The work you are about to do to improve your current life circumstances after reading this book will be worth its weight in gold. I promise that your results will be substantial and so very precious.

Working on yourself is the most valuable thing you will ever do, and I am deeply grateful for being a part of your journey, so thank you.

I will be writing this book as if I were having a conversation with my younger self and I will be explaining to you what I wish someone would have told me years ago. Although, I do truly believe in three things; 1, we have a path set out for us 2, timing is key and 3, there is always a beautiful lesson to be learnt in every experience ... both the good and the bad. Even though my life has had a lot of trauma and darkness, it has also had a lot of light and beauty. I would not change any part of it for the world.

After trauma comes the opportunity to heal. After unhappiness comes the determination to reach happiness.

After being mistreated and disrespected comes gaining your own personal strength and valuing yourself. After failure comes fighting towards success. If we choose so.

I am guessing the reason why this book crossed your path is that you have reached a point in your life where you want more. You want the answers. You want to heal. You want to move on from your past traumas. You want to be genuinely happy. You want to be successful in your relationships and in your career. You want to feel more positive. You want to have unwavering, deep-rooted confidence. You want to remove the anxiety and the self-sabotage.

Could you imagine achieving everything that you have ever wanted? Imagine how your life would be if you entertained your potential as much as you entertained your self-doubt. Could you imagine what it would feel like to wake up every day feeling genuinely happy? Grateful? Loved? Knowing that the Universe has always got your back? Could you imagine what it would feel like to finally move on from your previous traumatic experiences? To finally heal from everything and everyone that has ever hurt you. To have the ability to be able to trust people again. How empowering would it feel to finally feel in control of YOU?

Think how amazing it would feel to be free from the crippling anxiety and to be able to ignore all of the negative self-sabotage talk in your head. How about being completely resilient to everyone's negative bullshit and making YOUR life incredible. How would you feel and how different would your life look like if you developed a true, unshakeable self-confidence? I am here to tell you that after you read this book, this will all be your new normal ... and then some!

Unlike many self-help books you read, I'm not going to sit here and tell you that I have the right to write this book because I have a billion-pound business, that I don't have anything negative happen to me in my life, that I have seven figures in my bank account and that I visit ten exotic destinations via my private jet each year. However, what I am going to say is that I am extremely happy, content, optimistic, motivated, passionate, truly loved and I do adore my life. I am going to tell you that I have been through hell, and I have come out of the other side. I have healed from my past trauma. Please don't forget that I am also forever growing, evolving, and improving as situations unravel, and life unfolds.

So, the reason for me writing this book for you is to put all of that past pain and suffering into something productive and worthwhile. To make it all worth it. I was put through the trauma and the life I have lived so I could do something substantial with it and help others that need it.

Yes, I do wish that I knew everything in this book many years ago, but the reality is that we are exposed to what we need at **exactly the right time**. I have gathered and collected this knowledge over many years, which has brought me to this exact point in my life, so that I can now gift it to you, and you can implement it into your life. I would not have been ready to write this book before this exact moment ... but now is the right time. The right time for me to share this information with you and the right time for you to receive and act on it.

Happiness and success are as individual as a fingerprint. Someone's ideal happiness and goal in life may be to get divorced, to live alone in the middle of nowhere with no WIFI and grow their own vegetables. Someone else's dream may be to marry someone, to be with that person for the rest of their life and home school their children in the South of France. Someone else may want to be completely committed to their career, be a CEO, and have ten dachshunds in a high-rise apartment in New York City. Whatever your happiness and success looks like in your mind, I'm here to tell you that it is achievable for you.

I went from a less-than-ideal childhood in a broken home, to an even worse young adulthood which I will go into in more detail throughout the following chapters. I sought out to find the road to recovery, the ability to heal and to find my happiness during my mid to late twenties. I wanted to fully understand why I was like how I was. What caused it and more importantly, HOW I could change it. I started reading self-help books, having counselling, hypnotherapy, taking medication, trying meditation, having reiki healing sessions and basically a lot of self-questioning.

Achieving success and happiness to me was something that I never thought I would attain before, but luckily, after healing and growing, I now not only believe that it is possible, I believe that I deserve it. And so do you.

If I can go from being anxious, unhappy, having insomnia, being broke, alcoholism, angry, paranoid, and pessimistic to happy, content, motivated, loved, in control, passionate, positive, and optimistic, then so can you (believe me!).

To me, that alone is success. I was fighting for survival since I was a child, and I have learnt lessons from experiences that I never should have been forced to face. Which I have no doubt that you have too and that is exactly why you are reading this book right now.

We deserve to be free from that pain. We deserve to live a successful, content, and peaceful life surrounded by true love. We have earned it!

I started reading self-help books about nine years ago and since then, I have read hundreds. Many of their messages are similar, however, authors explain things in their own way. This means that even if you too have read hundreds of self-help books, I may explain something to you in a way that may finally work for you and just 'click'.

Plus, I have always thought that even if you learn just one new thing from a new self-help book, it was worth the read right?

When I gained all of this precious knowledge it completely transformed my life. I want that for you. I will explain to you absolutely everything that I wished someone told me years ago. Your life will start to dramatically improve as soon as you read this book and start putting all of it into practice ... that I can promise! It will genuinely feel like you have suddenly just woken up from a long, deep sleep.

So, whether you are new to all of this or you just want to expand your already broad knowledge on self-help, you will benefit from reading this book.

I will explain how to completely change your mind-set by being conscious of your thoughts and emotions. How to move on from your past traumas. How to get exactly what it is that YOU want in life and not just what society says you should have.

I will help you to gain a deep-rooted self confidence that no one can take away from you. I'll help you to remove the crap that you do not want in your life, including the negative self-talk, self-sabotage, anxiety, and anyone who messes with your vibe.

I will touch on the incredible benefits of spiritualism, meditation, crystals, your personal energy, Chakras, Reiki healing and even arm you with your own spiritual tool kit!

I will also hit you with the scientific facts as to why you currently are how you are. That way you can begin to heal yourself and learn how to not only gain, but also maintain, the incredible life that you deserve.

So, get comfortable, keep an open mind, and get ready to change your life for the better. You are about to see how every bad experience and detour you have gone through has led you to exactly where you needed to be. Right here. Are you ready? Let's go ...

CHANGE

A New and Improved Self

In any single moment you can choose to change. You can choose what or whom you have in your life. You can choose to stop allowing the pain and negativity from your past prevent you from living your fullest life right now. You are the only one who has this control and ability. Once you take this power back and apply it to your life, you will wish that you had done it so much sooner.

For change to happen, you must first be prepared to go outside of your comfort zone as this is where the true magic will happen. I'm not going to say it will be easy, but the rewards will be profound. To simply wish for a better life without putting any work into making it happen is, unfortunately, never going to give you the results that you deserve. I once read that the definition of insanity is doing the same thing repeatedly and hoping for different results. So, living on autopilot and doing the same things over and over again, but still wishing for a different life, is only going to disappoint you.

We will dive deeper into thoughts and emotions later but one of the first things you need to do right this second is to simply be aware of your thoughts. Millions and millions of people are running on autopilot when it comes to their thoughts and what they think. Not to mention autopilot being in control of their daily, habitual, activities. Just by being aware and observing your thinking is extremely powerful. By doing this it then gives you the opportunity to consciously change your old thought patterns, and therefore your emotions.

Any emotions that you experience are the direct result of what you are thinking. So, this is reassuring knowledge that no one else has the power to make you feel a certain way in any given circumstances. It is your own personal thoughts and the MEANING that you give to any person or situation which gives them their power. You have had the control to give this power away, so you also have the control to take it back. Once you start being consciously aware of your thinking and your emotions and realise that you have the power to adapt these, you can then begin to change.

How do you really feel about change? Ask yourself and answer with complete honesty. Many people try and do all they can to stay within their comfort zone, despite the fact that they will always remain in the same place in life if they do so. Many people feel really uneasy about any kind of change in their life because they fear the unknown. When in fact, if you want to improve any areas of your life, you have got to get pretty used to the idea of change. Change needs to be your new best friend from now on. The idea of change needs to excite you and scare you, simultaneously.

If you truly did not want to or need to change your life right now, you wouldn't be reading this book. You are showing that you are ready for a positive life-transformative change. So, let's welcome the change and embrace it. Progress is impossible without change. It may make you feel uncomfortable at first but what will be more painful is staying stuck somewhere that you do not want to be.

For a new and improved Self, you need to start thinking about what that really looks like for you. What do you see coming into your life? What do you see leaving it? How will you be feeling internally when you have reached your desired goal? This is your journey so you can have exactly what it is that you want. You can feel exactly the way that you desire to feel. You just have to start making some positive changes, internally and externally.

It's Going to Get Ugly Before It Gets Beautiful

Evolving as a person, finally facing your traumatic past, healing your old wounds, changing your daily 'habits' and manifesting everything that you have ever wanted is sometimes going to be hard. Only a few weeks ago my Google search history looked like this; 'Is it normal to cry during meditation?' 'Can you forgive people without them knowing and without letting them back into your life?' and 'Why is my heart so irregular two days after a reiki healing session?' Throughout this process, like I said, there will be highs and there will be lows. This is completely normal, expected, and actually, 100% needed. Shedding an old self that is stuck in pain and constantly running on auto-pilot in order to attract the person and life that you want, is not only liberating and scary, it is also essential. After this uncomfortableness you will finally find your true self, full of happiness and 'in flow'.

The dreaded term 'Shadow Work' is also unavoidable in this process. You will have to get really uncomfortable during some stages in order to dig up the old situations and emotions that you have had buried and suppressed for so long. And I get it, you have buried all of this for so many years in order to survive. I understand that it has been the only way that you have survived so much heartache and trauma in the past.

Now it is time to face it, acknowledge it, understand why we have done this, release it and then move on from it. There is no need to hold on to this negative side of ourselves anymore. It does not serve you anymore and it is now holding you back from living and experiencing everything that you have ever wished for. You owe this development and growth to yourself.

The benefits of shining light on these dark parts of ourselves that we have tried to hide and repress for many years are enormous, and trust me when I say, that by doing so, it will greatly improve every single area of your life. The communication and understanding you have with your loved ones will be so much more substantial. The relationships will become stronger, precious, and even more meaningful moving forward. You will gain a sense of control over your present life, and a sense of relief when visualising your future because you will understand that the past is over, and it can no longer harm you. The fears and anxieties about the future will diminish and fade when you understand that both the future and the past are simply illusions of the mind. You will develop a healthier way to understand yourself. You will begin to understand your emotions, your perceptions on everything and why you are how you are. As a result, once you begin this unpicking, you will start to develop such a newfound confidence that will then aid you in taking on new opportunities with open arms.

It will get difficult and ugly at times. The feeling of actively exposing ourselves to our painful past and questioning what we believe to be our current 'Self', of course can be overwhelming and make us feel vulnerable. You may even feel that you have gone backwards at times. However, these are important stages that need to happen for you to heal mentally, emotionally, and physically. This is when you will begin to resolve everything that has harmed you in the past. By doing so, you will no longer look backwards and fixate on the pain caused. Your daily habits will begin to be beneficial and constructive towards the future that you want to build for yourself. There can be so much beauty in the pain and hurt if it is resolved, healed and left where it should be, in the past.

It will get beautiful, and it will get incredible, I promise you. You will no longer feel trapped or like a prisoner of your past any longer. The hate you feel inside will melt away from you. Your body will begin to feel light again. You will have a healthy level of control over your own life again. The opportunities available to you will soon feel endless.

Beliefs – Just Because You Believe It, It Does Not Make It True

What I have noticed as I have grown older is that my old beliefs seem to, thankfully, be melting away. This has only happened through being aware of my destructive patterns and behaviours and continuously questioning myself. I remember before I met my fiancé, I believed down to my core that relationships never worked, and that marriage would always end in divorce. This belief was so strong that no previous relationship ever worked out, no matter how hard I had tried. During each failed relationship I had been in, consciously I was trying to be happy and make it work but my subconscious mind was on a whole different belief system.

My parents filed for divorce when I was just four years old. My first love cheated on me throughout our on and off toxic relationship, for over a decade. I had boyfriends that had secret lives they were hiding from me. I was about to let my guard down to one boyfriend in particular to tell him I loved him, only for him to cancel our date, go out on a lads night and get a girl pregnant …eventually moving her in. I have been emotionally destroyed, cheated on and lied to. I have also retaliated and been the mistress. I have snuck around with married men, not having a care for the wives because I had it done to me. I have been completely numb and disconnected with what I believed to be right and wrong.

I didn't start questioning my deep-rooted beliefs when it came to relationships until I met my fiancé, Andy. I actually remember a part of me realising that I didn't want to self-sabotage this relationship. Almost as if I knew I would ruin it from the get-go. So, I knew I had to put some work in and make some much-needed healthy changes in order for the relationship to even have a chance. We basically need to heal ourselves so that we can stop accidentally hurting the people that we want to love. Once we heal and stop projecting our own wounds on to them, we can then drop our guards and receive love safely.

I remember going into Waterstones and finding the book 'Healing Is the New High' by Vex King ... the timing could not have been any better. This book really opened my eyes to belief systems in particular and I finally began the process of unpicking my past. If you haven't already, you need to check it out.

I started questioning everything that I did and everything that I believed to be 'truth'. This was so incredibly liberating because I knew that positive changes were ahead! I would ask myself things like 'Why do I even believe that??' and 'Is that actually the truth or is that just what I believe to be true?'

Then I started to question if this was even a personal belief of mine or is this what I have been conditioned by others to be true. Many of our beliefs are not even our own! They stem from our childhood and what we were exposed to in our early years. Interestingly, these beliefs are what our parents and grandparents believed. So, in actual fact, until you are aware and question yourself, you may be sabotaging your own life because of past generational beliefs!

Realistically, marriages can work, and people can remain faithful. It just took me firstly, to be in the right mind-set and secondly, to actually start questioning that strong, imbedded, conditioned belief to finally see that clearly.

Sure, at first, to even begin bringing that wall and barrier down made me feel vulnerable, uncomfortable, and completely contrary to everything that I have previously believed. That will most likely be the case for you too. Eventually however, that feeling faded the more I reconditioned and enforced the new, healthy belief.

Another example of different views and belief systems, how do you feel about tarantulas? The likelihood is that you fear them, you would not want one anywhere near you and you certainly wouldn't dream of keeping one as a pet. Whilst we are over here hating on tarantulas, snakes and rats, there are people in the world out there that adore them. People that look after them for a living and have them all over their house as they love them so much. If you actually question your beliefs about tarantulas and try to see it through a tarantula-loving persons mind's eye, I bet you will realise that you could in fact think differently about them. I'm not saying you should, I'm just saying it's possible.

It is the same with dogs. Some people are petrified of dogs. They believe that they are aggressive, vicious, unpredictable and that they could start attacking you at any moment. Yet, someone else may believe that dogs are incredible, friendly, loyal, loving, pure and better company than most humans (because they are).

What I am trying to make you see is that, even with years of past experiences to support and back up our beliefs, they may not necessarily be beneficial to us … or even truth. One of the main reasons we are not where we want to be in life is because of our beliefs about our own capabilities.

Take a minute to question some of the things you believe to be true. Maybe you believe you can't leave your husband because you will be homeless and have no money to survive ... so you stay with him because you are frightened of life without that safety net. Maybe you believe you can't be successful because you have no qualifications or education, so you settle in your day-to-day job that makes you so unhappy. Maybe you believe that you are always going to have your particular illness because the doctor told you so. Maybe you believe all potential romantic partners are the same and you will eventually always get hurt ... so you stay single as you feel in control and safer that way.

Even if you believe these beliefs to your core, if they are detrimental to your life and your growth, they can be rewired and changed. If you have beliefs that do serve you and help your life to be fulfilled and happy, then great! But if they have a negative effect on you in any way, rest assure that we can change them.

When I started questioning my beliefs, it gave me the opportunity to actively choose new, healthier beliefs that would serve me. It brought my awareness to all of my old beliefs that were destructive and that I had been overlooking. I could then amend them for the better and reap the rewards as a result. This really helped me in all areas of my life, not just in my romantic relationships.

It helped me process and understand my lack of relationship with my Dad. My Dad never wanted a girl. He never knew how to communicate with me when I was young and still doesn't to this day (I'm 35 as I write this book). Luckily, my brother never felt this separation between himself and our Dad. After our parents had a divorce, me and my brother would visit my Dad every Sunday. This faded at the age of around twelve when I started realising how my Dad treated my Mum when they were together, and when I realised, we actually had nothing to talk about.

I remember a small memory I have of my Dad when I was around fourteen years old. We were driving in his big blue van on the way to his static home in Chichester. The song 'Walking Away' by Craig David came on as he was playing the album. I remember this one particular song bringing back good memories with my Dad. So, I must have taken my chances, wanting and needing some kind of closeness and love from him. Sat there in the car, I looked up to him as he was driving and I said to him, at the time confidently, 'What does this song make you think of?', knowing that we had shared a substantial memory and bond whilst listening to this song, and felt so sure that he would respond saying it reminded him of our time together. He replied with, 'This song reminds me of Jacqui (his girlfriend at the time). He followed on by saying 'I know you were hoping for me to say it reminds me of you and our happy times together, but it doesn't'.

Not long after that one of many truth-hitting scenarios, was another memory I have of receiving a birthday card from him. We were sitting around the dining table and I was handed a birthday card in an envelope from him. My friend, my Dads girlfriend at the time and her two sons and daughter were also around in the living room. I opened the card, and it read 'Happy Birthday, Love Steve'. Not Dad ... Steve. They could see my instant shock, confusion, and disappointment. He went on to make excuses and said, 'I was busy, and it was loud. There were loads of people here when I wrote it, I was distracted'. I was thirteen.

Although now I feel no hate towards him, I do feel indifferent. I'm not sure what would be worse for him to hear. I used to believe that it was his fault that we had no relationship. Until I started to understand that the reality was just a result of how he was conditioned as a child by his own father. His father had two sons and a daughter, and the same situation arose with my Grandad and Aunty. My Aunty never had a relationship with her Dad, and so, this is how he grew up ... not knowing how to have a father/daughter relationship. Seeing this as completely normal behaviour.

I am not excusing the behaviour because he hasn't been aware enough to change his own ways, however, I do understand that it is not his fault he was brought up around this. And, when you take it further, it's probably not even my Grandad's fault. This would more than likely be a long chain of subconscious, unawareness from past generations.

Waking up to and observing this pattern not only helps benefit your life but we also stop the pattern continuing down to our own children and the next generation. So, the benefits don't just stop with you. Questioning our beliefs and our views on other people and understanding why they are how they are, unlocks our own freedom and allows us to move forward without negativity.

Let us look at other areas of our lives. Do you believe that you can start the new business idea that you have had for so long? Do you believe that you can be successful and have whatever you want in life? Do you believe that you can lose the weight? Do you believe that you can be in a happy, healthy relationship that heals you and makes you a better person? If you don't believe any of this then it is time to start questioning WHY you don't believe it. Question why you have that particular negative belief that has been holding you back in life and ask if it is in fact, 'truth'.

Once you understand that you can change your old beliefs and rewire your brain to a new set of beliefs, everything will feel lighter. You will start seeing situations in a completely different light. You will begin to change for the better, both internally and externally.

One little reminder to get clear right now before we move on, is that you are allowed to talk about what they did to you and how it hurt you. It does not matter how they feel about you talking about it, because really, if they wanted people to think better of them, they should have been better. We do not have to shy away from our abusers and keep quiet just to make them feel comfortable. The goal is to **heal** from the past hurt and to **forget** the past hurt. By doing this, we can begin to live a happy and healthy life **without** carrying that hurt. Use that pain as motivation to finally remove it from your being.

Change Is the Only Way to Transform

There is a version of you ten years from now, that is begging this current version of you to start working on healing from the past, and to put in the work to change and evolve.

Many self-help books will tell you that in order to get a better life, all you will have to do is stick up pictures of the things that you want to manifest on a wall and write down that you're thankful and grateful for the new million-pound yacht sitting outside your house. But I am here to tell you, unfortunately that is not the case. There is a lot more to it.

Although it is great to have visuals up and around your home and in your daily life to help manifest, there are other areas you need to work on. I am a very visual person; I even made a mock-up of this very book you are holding before it was published. I did it when manifesting Leo, my dachshund. I had stuffed toy dachshunds around the house and a camera roll full of them on my phone. It certainly helps if you are as visual as me, but like I said, that is just the tip of the manifesting iceberg.

To transform your world for the better, deep-rooted changes are necessary. If you are unhappy with something ... change it. We think that because we live where we live, because we are in the relationship that we are in, or because we have been in that dead-end job for years, it means that it must remain that way ... when actually, that is far from the truth. You can go anywhere, do anything and be with/without whoever you choose. The moment you start to get out of your comfort zone is the moment you will become happier. Life will flow with you and not against you. You are not a tree. This is something I tell myself, my friends, and my family very often. You are not a tree. You do not have to stay in one position your whole entire life.

After you do the internal work and make some of these changes for yourself, let me tell you, you will naturally want to do it for other people you care about. The frustration I have felt over the years at friends and family who are stuck in negative situations because they fear change and have zero self-confidence.

Unfortunately (and fortunately) change is a personal inside job that no one else can do for you. If you try to change people, you will either push them away or end up being frustrated by your failed efforts. Of course, we can give our best advice and offer guidance, however, you can't change people who do not see anything wrong with their way of living (no matter how much they may moan about it). You can tell your best friend until you are blue in the face to leave her terrible partner, but only she can make that decision and act upon it herself. You can tell your family member to quit their dead-end job and to go for their dream in a new business venture, but again, only they can make that move for themselves.

What we can do however, is choose to *accept* that this is the way they are. We can allow them to simply be that way. Once we do this, we can use our power to *decide* if we want to stress ourselves out when they don't want to receive our help, or we can change ourselves and how we perceive the situation.

What is most important is that YOU can make these positive changes for YOU. When they eventually do ask you why your life has dramatically changed for the better and why you are so happy and successful now, you can tell them how you did it, and then, hopefully, it will inspire them to begin their own journey into unlocking their unlimited potential.

During this transformation, no doubt those same people will say to you, 'You've changed', and that is when you will respond with, 'We're meant to'. We cannot become what we want by remaining what we are. Change isn't meant to be easy. It is meant to rip up our roots and put us in new soil, where our roots can deepen and fully flourish. It might not feel 'OK' temporarily, but the evolution will eventually feel incredible.

Every time you level up, you will lose something. A bad habit, a fake friendship, an old toxic version of yourself. But that is not loss. That is just proof you are evolving. Our backgrounds may have had a huge influence on who we currently are, but we are responsible, and more importantly, in control, of who we are going to become.

In upcoming chapters, we will dive in deeper and work together on how to change our neural pathways, which will therefore transform our internal and external worlds. But I will leave you with this quote on change to keep in mind.

'Yesterday I was clever, I wanted to change the world. Today I am wise, so I am changing myself' - *Rumi*

HEALING FROM PAST TRAUMA

Triggers

Have you ever been triggered by something which made you feel furious, paranoid, sad or petrified pretty much instantly, without a second thought? Even if the person or situation in front of you was completely safe and had no real direct threat to you at all? Maybe you have even realised that you had been overly dramatic in your reaction? Leaving you with a sense of guilt, regret, and disappointment immediately after your automatic outburst. But at the time, you had basically no control over your thoughts and emotions because they were overwhelmingly strong. It was just such a natural reaction, right?

Anything that triggers us is teaching us exactly what part of ourselves that needs healing. Many people experience daily triggers that remind them of the past traumatic events that they have been through, which they unfortunately experienced against their will. A veteran may experience flash backs of the horrific events that they witnessed during war, when a nearby family innocently enjoys fireworks. A woman may close-up emotionally when being intimate with her partner because she was once brutally raped or mistreated. She may push her partner away because the thought of being open with anyone just reminds her of the vulnerability and pain she encountered. Someone may get instantly defensive and shout at their partner just because they slightly raised their voice at them. This would take them right back to an earlier toxic relationship that always resulted in intense, verbally abusive arguments.

Our brains have been wired to keep us safe in any situation, that is one of its many important and beneficial jobs. I'm sure you know the fight or flight sensations the mind and body both produce simultaneously to protect ourselves.

At the beginning of time, it would help us hunt to eat and run to survive. Nowadays (for people without PTSD) it is more of a, 'Don't walk alone down a dark alleyway in a bad neighbourhood', or 'Don't get involved with that person because they are known to cheat' kind of vibe. For PTSD sufferers it goes a hell of a lot deeper than that.

When the brain produces the fight or flight response, it activates the sympathetic nervous system. This triggers the extra release of hormones cortisol and adrenaline, and therefore causes physical changes and sensations in the body. Now, this is great if there is actual danger in front of you, however, if you have been through a traumatic past experience and are triggered daily (or most days), this can be detrimental to your physical and mental health. Crippling anxiety, depression, and insomnia are extremely common ...

as well as broken relationships and a lack of focus and concentration.

When I was around seventeen, my life was already crumbling around me, I was unable to live at home due to my Mum's partner at the time. He was a verbally abusive, unemployed, drug addict, and narcissistic. My then on/off first love was cheating on me and breaking my heart continuously. I couldn't live with any other family members, so I was living with a work colleague of mine in Brighton. With nothing to lose, I decided to up and move to Greece to work from the March to the October for an active holiday group.

That is when my situation unfortunately deteriorated. I had an accident in the work accommodation one morning before my shift. After showering, I slipped and fell off the concrete step on to the wet kitchen tiled floor. Two hours from the nearest hospital, my head was bleeding out on to the floor, I was seeing flashing lights in my vision, and I thought I wasn't going to make it. After a two-hour drive in the back of my managers car around the Greek coastal mountains, which felt like a lifetime, I finally arrived at the hospital. My manager couldn't stay with me, so there I was, alone in a Greek hospital. No friends or family. Surrounded by people that didn't even speak my language, coming at me with needles, glue, and staple guns. I spent the next four days in that hospital, not really knowing if I was going to be OK or not. They stapled my head, glued it, and sent me back to the hotel resort. About a week after that, I developed a health anxiety and a travel anxiety which I wasn't to know would last for the next 16 years ...

After not sleeping for five days straight after returning from the hospital, the company I worked for decided to fly me back home to Sussex, England, to stay with my Mum. I remember her stroking my hair with my head on her lap on the sofa to try and help me sleep. I started to feel as though I was going insane. I spent weeks in bed, thinking that if I were to get up and shower, I would die.

Eventually I built up the courage and forced myself to try and live a normal life again, but the anxiety was intensely crippling. I constantly believed that I was going to die. I thought I was about to have a stroke, I thought I had a brain tumour, I thought I was going to have a heart attack. You name it, I believed it was going to happen. I genuinely believed these thoughts and that the (insert horrific health episode here) was happening right now. So, you can imagine my fight or flight response was on constant overdrive.

I remember a time when I was driving down a busy road, and suddenly, an intrusive anxiety thought popped into my head that I was going to stop breathing. I saw two strangers across from me on the other side of the road, so I drove through the oncoming traffic, got out of the car, and ran up to them asking for help. I couldn't breathe. Luckily, they took me into their home and calmed me down until my Aunty came to help.

After years of this ruining my daily life and subconsciously imbedding new negative belief systems into my brain, I started calling the doctors multiple times a day with new symptoms. Anything from flashing lights in my vision, to ice pick headaches, to irregular heartbeats, to tingling sensations ... you name it, I called the doctor about it. I called the on-call doctors and had face to face appointments multiple times a week. They eventually referred me to counselling sessions which I attended twice a week, for about eight months. I learnt about anxiety and what it does to your mind and your body. I knew why my brain was doing it and I understood how the brain was affecting my physical body. I learned the subject of anxiety inside and out. I could lecture anyone on the facts about anxiety ... but to stop the anxious thoughts and the physical panic attacks for an extended period of time? I just could not do it.

I tried meditation, I tried hypnotherapy, I tried another five months of counselling for PTSD specifically, nothing helped. This was the part of my life where I started drinking heavily, I started stripping to make money and I had terrible insomnia. When I did eventually sleep, I would have horrific vivid nightmares ... and then sleep paralysis as like a cherry on the top.

The doctors eventually prescribed me Propranolol, which is a beta-blocker. They are designed to stop the physical panic attacks by preventing the heart to race, so I could physically live my day-to-day life. Sure, they stopped the physical attacks, but they didn't stop the internal mental anxiety-ridden thoughts about dying, and the paranoia of having something wrong with me. This merry-go-round lasted until I was about 25 (which I will go into more detail with you later).

Other than the health anxiety, as I mentioned, I also developed a travel anxiety. I began to genuinely believe that if I were to travel more than 30 minutes away from my home, something terrible would happen to me, and I would die. I understand how ridiculous that sounds to someone without a travel anxiety, but to me, this was a real danger at the time. This made life extremely restricting as you can imagine. It was at this stage that I understood I needed more substantial help other than the counselling and medication, because they were just not cutting it. So, I started researching other ways to help myself.

I remember a stripper friend of mine recommended a book called 'The Secret' by Rhonda Burnes. When she first described the book and the concept to me, and how you must be optimistic and manifest good outcomes, I thought she was deluded and far away from reality. If only I knew then what a significant positive impact that book was to have on my life.

It was a real turning point. I finally felt like I was awake, aware, and able to see the light at the end of a dark tunnel. I was, and still am, obsessed with that book. I have bought it for all my friends and family ... and anyone I meet that I believe could receive help from reading it.

During the 2020 covid pandemic, I had another turning point when I decided to finally come off the prescribed medication for the health anxiety. I decided to reduce the daily dose of the beta-blockers I was taking, as I felt I didn't need to be on them anymore. The doctor gave me the go ahead and recommended that I could deduct one tablet per week, over four weeks. Great, I thought ... however, it was not until summer 2024 that I fully stopped taking the medication and it was finally out of my system. I had to do this slowly to help my mind process the thought of being without them. My safety net was leaving from under me, so I took my time with the process so I could remain as comfortable as possible. I went from one tablet per day, to a half per day, to a half every other day.

We need to realise that it does not matter how long something takes us or how slowly we think we are going. If we are making progress and taking positive steps to move forward, that is all that matters. You need to look at the first step, not the whole staircase.

Coming off the tablets after thirteen years was both tough and incredibly empowering. I fought through a full month worth of withdrawal symptoms, thinking that I was not strong enough to come off them. I remember being so hard on myself, thinking that I had gone right back mentally to where I was when I was 22. To now, being a year with no anxiety medications and in control when the panic and anxiety does arise. It's important to understand that although we may never be completely free from the anxiety itself, we can learn to not allow it to affect us and ruin our lives. Leaving us with a new sense of self-achievement and the courage to face our fears.

I suppose the real reason why I am explaining this medication and health anxiety journey to you in such detail, is to show you just how powerful your thoughts are, and how many years one traumatic experience can negatively affect our lives. I am in no way saying that you should come off any medication you may be on right now, but what I am saying is that medications just simply mask the issues and prolong the real healing. Just like pain killers only mask the pain temporarily. What I am hoping is that when you do become aware of this, you may have a different consultation at your next doctor's appointment.

What Is Actually Happening to The Brain

We have two sides to our brain, the left, which oversees language, speaking, reading, writing, decision making ...

basically anything analytical, and the right side, which is in control of visuals, art, music, emotions, humour ... basically anything creative.

A critical piece of knowledge to learn and understand is what is actually happening to your brain when you are being triggered. By doing this, we take away the power of what is triggering us, and we remain the one in control ...so we can live a happier and pain free life moving forward.

Brain scans have shown that when we are in a present situation that reminds us of a traumatic past experience, the left side of the brain literally shuts itself down, and the right side of the brain is then dominant. This means that in that exact moment, our brains are literally re-living the original traumatic experience right then and there. We have no sense of the time gap between what happened back then and what is happening right now in front of us. So, people who suffer with PTSD are in fact continuously living their horrific experience ... in real time.

Knowing this and what is happening to your brain will help when you feel anxious about driving down that certain road you once were involved in a car crash on, or when you get paranoid that your new partner is going to cheat on you and treat you exactly like your ex did.

Understanding what the brain is doing is key and a huge step in recovery. When you start being aware of the PTSD and triggering process, you can then begin to create a new way of thinking, by being in the now and the present moment. A new neural pathway will begin to form and eventually you will change your behaviour and responses to these situations. I highly recommend the book, 'The Body Keeps the Score', written by Bessel Van Der Kolk. In this book Kolk explains how trauma literally reshapes our minds and our bodies. He discusses, in detail, what happens to us when we are triggered and how to reclaim our lives back. His book was, and still is, a significant help to me and my ability to heal from my past, so I strongly suggest you invest in his book too.

Sharing this information on triggers and trauma to family, friends and partners will also be a huge help in the healing process, because they will also understand why you are reacting the way that you do. This is definitely something I wish I knew years ago, and it is still currently helping me with my relationships, when I am driving or flying, and when my health anxiety develops a new 'symptom'.

A New Conscious Behaviour

So far, in the past two chapters alone, you have learnt the most effective ways to begin your journey to a new and improved life, filled with happiness, contentment, health and love. Just through being aware of your thoughts and understanding how your brain is working when you are being triggered, you have the code to now unlock a new way of thinking so you can rewire new conscious behaviours.

After realising that my old ways of thinking restricted me from going anywhere further than 30 minutes from my home, I read about exposure therapy and decided to push through my comfort zone to dissolve this particular mental health issue.

When I met my fiancé Andy, I not only wanted to change my belief system when it came to romantic relationships and trust, I also wanted to change my belief that something terrible would happen if I ventured away from my home. Andy's work takes him all over Europe and America. When we met, he was moving to Las Vegas. Now this would be a test! Considering I had difficulty even driving the hour trip to the airport, the thought of then flying ten hours across the world physically and mentally petrified me.

I remember walking along the beach with my Mum and saying to her, 'If I don't push myself to do this, I will be stuck in Worthing my whole life'. I have always tried to explain to loved ones how I feel like I have two people inside my mind. One voice is completely strong, determined to do anything and CAN do anything! The other is anxious, paranoid, and would probably be quite happy curled up on the sofa in cottonwool all day with the dog … not doing anything.

For many years this second voice would dominate the first, but after being aware that I have the power to change my world, I decided to start listening to the stronger, more determined voice. I started to push through my comfort zones. I would purposely put myself in these anxious situations just to prove to myself that a, I can do it, and b, nothing bad would happen to me when I did. I was rewiring my brain and creating a new reality. By consciously doing this repeatedly, I went to visit Las Vegas two times before I eventually moved here, with my dog, in 2023 (we will go into that in more detail later!).

When you continuously act consciously, you imbed a new neural pathway into your brain. In time, these will eventually be the new, healthier habits and therefore become your new beliefs.

The only way to attempt to dissolve the anxiety and the irrational fear is by exposing yourself to the anxiety and triggers, and not by avoiding them. That thought alone may seem terrifying but hear me out ... when we take the control away from what makes us anxious and actively make the decision to expose ourselves to it, repeatedly, we do two things. Firstly, we diminish the power and size of the situation at hand that we so desperately fear. Secondly, if practiced regularly, we continue to make the issue smaller and smaller each time. So eventually, it will become known that it is safe in our minds because it continuously did not result in any danger. When you repeatedly use exposure therapy, you will start to trust yourself, your own capabilities, and the Universe. Avoiding your triggers is not healing. It is making them even more substantial and strong. Healing happens only when you are triggered and you are able to move through the pain, the pattern, the old story, and walk your way to a new positive ending.

One major problem is that people avoid learning about anxiety as a subject ... let alone their own specific anxieties that they may have. This means by not understanding anxiety and how it can potentially be helped, they just believe that nothing can be done about it and, 'It's just how they are now'. Knowledge will definitely become your power when it comes to diminishing your unwanted anxiety.

How many times have you thought something bad was going to happen to you? With a flight? With your partner going out? When you go to meet a large group of people or when you have had to do an important speech? ... How many times have you had a panic attack? And how many times did you survive it? You have survived every single worst day you have ever experienced, that is a fact.

Healing Is an Ongoing Job

Like I said before, working on yourself is the most valuable thing you will ever do, and it should be a subject that we never stop learning and developing. Our worlds internally and externally are our own masterpieces that should never be seen as fully complete, up until the day that we die. Healing from past trauma is never going to be plain sailing. It will be smooth some days and then painfully difficult other days ... and that is OK. Both you and your support network must be patient and trust the process.

When you have bad days and you feel as though you are going backwards, potentially undoing the healing that you have accomplished, just look back and review what has not gone quite to plan. Ask yourself what you can do differently to improve the situation moving forward, so it does not repeat itself again.

A few weeks ago, just a normal day living here in Las Vegas, I thought I would pop in the car and drive fifteen minutes to the supermarket. Just a normal task that had no serious danger whatsoever. I got into the car and when I reached just five minutes away from my home, I had an overwhelming feeling of anxiety hit me. Without my anxiety medication safety net. My heart was racing and thumping, and I could not control my breathing. I was trying to remain calm so I could safely drive, but I expected the worst to happen.

I resorted to calling my Mum through the car speaker system. 5000 miles away, I was crying and panicking down the phone to her. In that moment I had two options ... I could either U turn and go home, which let's face it, felt like the safer and easier choice at the time, or I push through the panic, observe the anxiety from a detached point of view rather than fight it, and carry on to the supermarket. I KNEW what my brain was doing, I knew it was putting me right back in a dangerous situation when I was completely safe. So, I started telling myself exactly that, aloud. I was talking to myself in the car, telling myself that I was safe, that I was in control, that I did not have to be anxious anymore. I was almost trying to reassure my anxiety trauma like it was a friend, and not the enemy.

I managed to get to the supermarket that day, but I was still so frustrated and disappointed in myself that I got to that level of fear. So, laying in bed that night, I decided that the very next day I would re-write the experience I had that day. And I did exactly that. I got into the car and I drove the same route to the store, just to prove to myself that I could do it with no anxiety this time. I got to the store, parked up into the car park as I didn't need anything ... and I just sat there and cried. I had such a sense of relief. I felt empowered and in control, finally. This may seem so silly and so small to some people, but to me, this was huge. Alone in Las Vegas, 5000 miles away from England, off my beta blockers, experiencing anxiety attacks again, but thinking no, I am going to re-write that previous day's setback, and I am going to write a new story. It was no longer going to beat me and have a hold over me.

You may have to re-write your bad days when you are healing and evolving, but that just means we are growing. We are becoming aware. It means we are changing for the better. It means we are finally recovering from the trauma. May you find so much peace that it becomes almost impossible to trigger you.

GET RID OF WHAT YOU DON'T WANT

Get Prepared to Cut off the Dead Wood

Before receiving the life of your dreams, you must first remove anything and everything in your life right now that does not enhance you as a being, bring you love and happiness, or anything that prevents you from growing.

Please don't just skim over this part of the process because you believe, 'It is how it is', 'I can't just remove them from my life' or 'I can't quit this job' because believe me a, you can and b, it's essential. This is where you will have to start being ruthless in removing anything that does not serve you.

Your future happiness depends on it. The courage it takes to leave behind what is not for you anymore, is the same amount of courage that will push you to find what is meant for you.

In order for you to find the dream partner, find the perfect well-paid and fulfilling job, and find the ideal city to live in that makes you thrive, you must make the room for it.

Everything that you have ever dreamt of will only begin to materialise as a reality in your life once you have removed and/or made the room for it. Only when there is room, will the Universe align and fulfil that desire for you. This is because you are finally telling the Universe that you are ready to receive it all.

Have you ever watched an episode of Hoarders? A person has collected items for multiple years which has resulted in their home being inhabitable, to say the least. They believe that each object that they hold on to will someday serve a purpose, or it means something special to them. Even if it is a load of empty plastic bottles they have owned for 15 years. They have created an attachment and a meaning to these items, even though they can't be used due to the fact that they have been hidden under a huge pile of other items for so long.

A hoarder's home is very much like our lives. The items within the home are our thoughts, the people around us, and our circumstances. In order to have a healthy and content home (or life) with only useful and meaningful items within it, we have to first declutter, deep clean, and then redecorate. This way we can eventually have a beautiful happy and functionable home.

When you start to declutter life, the entire process will initially feel like you are letting go of 'important' things, and it may even seem like you are removing your safety net from underneath you. What you must keep in mind throughout this part of the process is the fact that if it does not bring you happiness, it must go. We have only one life. Your precious time and energy must be spent only on the people and the experiences that bring out the absolute very best of you.

Just because they are related to you, that does not mean they deserve to still be a part of your life. Just because you are currently married to them, if they make your life hell, it does not mean that you have to stay married with that person. Just because you think you can't get a better job because you have no education or qualifications, it does not mean that you have to stay in a job that makes you miserable, anxious and feel worthless.

The people you do remove or lose during your healing process are the people that are only meant to be associated with the unhealed version of you. Not everyone and everything must continue with you into your new chapter.

Once you have decided on the things in your life that do not propel you forward and add to your happiness and wellbeing, it is time to act. By doing this, you will naturally be making room for the things that you truly do desire. You will be clearing out and making the mental, emotional, and physical space ready for the Universe to bring you exactly what it is that you want and need. Remember, some things are meant to happen but not meant to be.

You'll Naturally Filter Out the Bad and Be Left with the Good

My current life is a million miles away from my earlier life, and I don't just mean geographically. From the age of 18 to around 24, I was at the worst stage of my life. I was stripping, I was an alcoholic, I never slept, I had horrific anxiety, I had sex with men for money, I had no true friends and I was in and out of toxic relationships. The negativity and self-sabotage list was endless.

Now, I don't usually share this old version of myself to people I just meet, let alone to potentially millions of people around the world (plus let's face it, my family and friends are going to read this) but I think it is so important that I am 100% honest and open with you.

By doing so, you can see just how much is possible for you once you make the necessary changes in your life. Especially if you are on a downward spiral and unhappy. By me being completely transparent and open with you, I am hoping that you can really understand the value of removing what makes you unhappy, changing your old belief systems, healing from your traumas and manifesting the life you want.

When I hit my rock bottom, I was drink driving to and from work at a strip club in Brighton. The recession had hit the UK so I would be lucky if I left the club £20 in profit, what with the house fees, the money I spent on alcohol to get through the night, and the petrol getting there.

I remember when I couldn't even afford toilet roll so I would have to take some from the nearby public toilets. My Aunty would have to drop me over some tampons when I was on my period. I had no gas supply to my flat to be able to cook, and eventually my car was towed away as I had no money to pay for the tax, insurance, and an MOT. Let alone put petrol in it to move the thing! Top that off with constant crippling anxiety, sleep paralysis and insomnia, bailiffs knocking at my door and someone I loved mentally and emotionally abusing me.

I am not shameful about the situation I was in. I didn't have anyone to help and support me. So, I had to fend for myself and pull myself out of the dark hole. I will always hold my head up high when explaining the truth about my past and this chapter. I had no other options at the time (given the mindset I had) and I needed a way to survive.

Meeting and having sex with men for money was what paid for my food, put a roof over my head, and essentially pulled me out from what could have been the end of my life. To this day I hear about the outcome of the other strippers I worked with at the time. Some have committed suicide, some are addicted to drugs, and some are still in the game.

At the age of 25, I started reading self-help books as I knew that was not the life I wanted to continue to live, and I knew deep down that I was destined for so much more. I decided, if I wanted to get myself out of that life and enter my happy era, I had to remove everything that I did not want in my life. Then I had to start manifesting the life that I did want. That is when my life finally started to blossom. I had a great job in recruitment, I was drinking alcohol but like a normal human being, I manifested a lot of money, designer shoes, bags, clothes, laptops, jewellery, a flat full of beautiful things. I entered the world of modelling, which was an amazing, healthy hobby. I built a huge social media following, a modelling website to bring in some revenue, and I even created a business plan and started my own online lingerie store.

When you finally decide you are worth more and want more than your current situation, when you act upon and do yourself the honour of saying goodbye to the people, situations and things that have a negative impact on you, miracles WILL start to happen.

We became who we needed to become in order to survive our past. Now it is our time to become who we need to be to thrive in our future.

Choose What Your 'Tunnel Vision' Is On

Now we have removed everything that does not deserve to be in our precious world moving forward, we now need to start choosing what our tunnel vision is focused on. This is probably where the negative thinkers in your life will start to notice a dramatic change in you, and more than likely, the trash is going to start to take itself out.

Imagine for a second that you are inside of a transparent glass tunnel. Withing this glass tunnel, you are actively creating the perfect environment for yourself. You are doing the work and you are moving forward, positively. When you become aware of your thoughts, and you are consciously beginning to focus on the positives that surround you, internally and externally, you are going to notice a lot of negatives trying to mess with your vibe. These will be like arrows trying to attack you within this glass tunnel. The aim is to not allow them to reach you, and for them to bounce right back off the thick glass that you have surrounded and protected yourself with.

This may look like turning the TV off if the news is constantly reporting bleak events from the world in your home. It could mean you don't participate in a slagging match with your colleagues about your boss, who is actually pretty nice to you. It could mean that you try and change the subject to something more optimistic when you are out for dinner with a friend that is complaining about their useless partner or ill health. It could mean blocking and deleting that person's telephone number.

By eliminating the day-to-day pessimism, it will naturally create more of an optimistic outlook on your day. This will have a huge ripple effect on your week, month, and year.

Once you consciously do this, it will eventually become second nature to you. You will be so aware of other people's negativity that you will not want to be around them, and it will almost feel like there are dirty germs in the air that you don't want to breathe in.

I remember when I went to meet a friend for lunch at a local Italian restaurant in town. It was a beautiful summers day with a lovely cool breeze, so we sat outside to eat, drink, and catch up. All she spoke about throughout the entire lunch date was death, ill health in her family and a guy that was giving her the run around. After an hour of me trying to change the subject and trying to make her see the positives of what she was explaining, I had to say to her that I had to leave ... I couldn't take it anymore.

Her energy had affected my body so much that I couldn't even walk home properly. I lived just a 10-minute walk through town from the restaurant. It was such an overwhelming feeling that my body and legs just stopped working. I had to call my Mum and ask her how I was going to get back home. When I eventually did get back, I instantly dug out my white sage and burnt it. Not only throughout my home, but I covered myself in the smoke to try and clear away the energy that had attached on to me from the lunch date (We will go through white sage and other spiritual tools to help protect your energy in a later chapter).

Did you know that the hearts electromagnetic field reaches three to six feet away from our body? This is a scientific fact which I will discuss in more detail later in the book. So, when someone is being negative and has a draining energy right in front of you, it is not surprising that it effects your body and its energy negatively ... especially if you are someone who is sensitive to other people's energies.

Depending on my day and who I plan to see, I will wear a necklace or carry a crystal in my pocket or bag. Doing this will either attract positive energies or protect me from the negative ones. We will also delve deeper into the strong benefits of crystals in a later chapter.

'Definition of resilience' - The ability to withstand or to recover quickly from difficulties. Being resilient to harmful energy and situations takes huge strength, and also requires a conscious effort at first. By becoming resilient to external negative energy, you will be protecting your own internal energy with a necessary thick layer, and more importantly, only allowing positive energy to filter through to your core.

How to Deal with Roadblocks

Even if you eventually become a master at attracting all of the positive energy into your life and gain the ability to repel the negative, there will unfortunately be circumstances where undesirable things will happen to you, which you initially have no control over. This is where you will have to dig deeper and consciously respond and act, rather than erratically and instantly react. Once you master this you will be untouchable.

In 2018 when my life was finally on track, I was continuously becoming highly successful, and I was attracting everything positive in my life ... I was struck with an obsessive stalker. During this time, I had a huge social media following of around 500,000 collectively across all platforms. I was having photoshoots with photographers, and I was collaborating and creating content for companies. Not only was l creating content for social media platforms, but I was also creating content for a subscription-based website that I had built for myself. This website attracted hundreds of subscribers that each paid a monthly fee to unlock all of my content. Little did I know that just one of those individuals was about to bring my life hell for the next seven years.

It began with this person sending direct messages to me like he was a personal friend, which of course, he was not. It then developed to him sending essay-long messages, multiple times a day which were a nuisance. After a while I politely explained that I would have to cancel his subscriptions due to the mass amount of contact from him, which was an inconvenience to receive each day. That is when he turned nasty and the fake profiles he created began to send me abuse.

I constantly had fake accounts attacking my posts publicly, as well as direct messages in my inbox, saying that I was the devil, I manipulated men and that I was no role model to younger women. I knew this was him by the lengths of the text and the incorrect spelling and grammar. Sure, this was annoying but luckily, I have a thick skin, and a simple delete/block would solve the problem. I thought.

My accounts were suddenly bombarded with reports and were deactivated by the providers. Accounts that took a huge amount of time and effort to build and were the only audience I had for my new lingerie business that I had just recently launched. Although I cannot confirm he was the cause of the accounts being reported and deactivated, the timing just seemed perfect ...

So, there I was, having only just received a small business loan to fund my lingerie business, and now no audience to sell to. I then began getting apologetic email essays from his own personal email account. Up until that point, the stalking had been online ... until I physically saw him in my local high street.

As I lived ten minutes from Worthing town, I would walk there daily, go to my office, the post office to ship lingerie, look around the shops, walk on the sea front, and go to the pier to read and have coffee ... then return home. Now, my eyesight is horrific, so I have no idea how many previous times he had seen me, but on this particular day he tried to approach me to apologise. I said to him right then and there, if he were to continue, I would get the police involved to enforce that he leaves me alone.

One night, a few weeks later, I was in bed with my bed side lamp on, reading a book. Suddenly, I could hear what I thought to be people talking outside the big bay window where my bed head was. At first, I didn't think too much of the voices as this was a driveway where my neighbours would regularly walk past to get to their front door. It was not until fifteen minutes had gone by that I realised the voice was still there, and it was just one, a male. I instantly had a gut feeling it was him. I turned my light off and got under the covers. The realisation hit me that only a thin sheet of glass was between my head and my stalker. He began mumbling and continuously coughing. Petrified, I got out of bed and went to my hallway, which was away from any windows, and I called the police. The first operator I spoke to said it could just be my neighbours ... she had no sense of urgency. I tried to explain to her what I did for a living and that I had an online stalker, whom I saw in town not that long ago. She was evasive but said that she would send a police car around.

A few quiet moments later, a tapping on the bedroom window began and my name was being whispered. My real name, Sam, not Tia, which was the name I went by when modelling. Completely paralysed as to what to do, I stayed in the hallway waiting for the police to come and help. I began texting my Mum for a sense of reassurance as she lived just a fifteen-minute drive away.

More time went by, and the police were still nowhere to be seen. The glass tapping then moved to my kitchen window

… and then my living room windows. He knew all the windows that were specific to my flat. How?? The male voice got louder and louder, calling my name. I called the police for a second time asking for them to send help, but nothing. I then asked my Mum to get in the car and pick me up so I could stay with her, as the police clearly were not coming. My flat door buzzer buzzes ... he knows which flat number I am.

Shortly after this, my Mum pulls up in the car across the road and tells me later that she saw a short man in a poncho, with short curly hair, pulling a suitcase, leaving the buildings driveway and started to walk down the road towards town.

I'm finally safe with my Mum, heading to her home in the car, but this whole ordeal from start to finish lasted around 40 minutes.

The very next morning I contacted my letting agency to explain what had happened and to tell them that I desperately needed to move, asap.

The police finally contacted me via telephone the following morning to take details as no one came to help me when I needed them.

Until I managed to move home, I cannot begin to describe to you the feelings of anxiety, vulnerability, and paranoia that I experienced. I did not feel safe inside my own home or being outside. I was trapped and suffocated. I was constantly watching my back when I was out, and I would always have my curtains closed and doors double locked when I was inside.

I eventually moved home six weeks later, and I instantly installed a video doorbell in fear of it happening again. The police eventually arrested the stalker, and he was interviewed. The officers told me that he had said he believed we were in a romantic relationship and that he loved me. The police investigator told me that he could clearly tell that this was not the case, and thankfully, they then began to be helpful and supportive towards me. With multiple visits from the Worthing investigator, he asked me what outcome I wanted from all of this. I said I didn't wish bad on him or for him to go to prison, but I needed him to listen to both myself and the police and to leave me alone.

The CPS issued him a five-year restraining order. The conditions were that he could not have contact directly or indirectly with me, he could not publish or post in any way, any material relating to me on any social media or on the internet in general, he could not go to my home address, be within 100 metres of Tia Mendez Boutique HQ (which was my office in Worthing town center) and he could not knowingly be within 100 metres of me.

I had hoped that the legal order would have put a stop to all of the contact from him and he would allow me to live my life in peace, however, unfortunately this was not the case. The contact from him continued soon after the restraining order was served, and it continued right up until the end of October 2023 when I announced my engagement with Andy.

He was constantly creating more fake profiles, he contacted my partner to 'warn' him off me when we first started dating, he contacted my friends, friends of Andy's and even Andy's boss. Saying things like I ruined his life with putting a restraining order on his record, that I was going to ruin Andy's life if Andy was not careful and that I was bad news. He actually said I was stalking and harassing him. He would email Andy with fake 'evidence' that he created, I'm guessing through photoshop apps, which included my images and fake captions he had added. He would make contact with potential business associates that I had lined up to try and sabotage my financial income. He threatened to have the restraining order removed and wanted to sue the police for not listening to him. He would also always make some kind of contact at every single special occasion, whether it was my birthday or an anniversary.

I could go into all of the details with every single breach of the restraining order he made, but I am sure by now, you can understand the extent of stress, anxiety, and ill mental health it caused.

The final straw for me was when I announced my engagement with Andy in October 2023. As a result of the engagement, he posted an essay-long text of a suicide threat on my Facebook post, stating that he was about to take his own life and that I was the reason for him doing so. I contacted the police straight away. I also had to file a complaint with them so they would actually listen and act on this matter. Thankfully, he was re-arrested.

Since then, myself and the people in my world have had no contact from him. The police seized his devices and sent them off for the CPS to review the breaches of restraining order and we are looking at extending the order indefinitely ... even if he is not sentenced and put into prison.

The whole experience was horrific. It caused me such trauma, however throughout everything, I have learnt that people and situations can be powerless without your reaction to them. I have learnt that I am strong. I have grown deeper love, trust and respect with both Andy and my friends and family. They have shown me unconditional loyalty. They have shown me that I am loved, and they have shown me they truly care for me.

What kept me going throughout this whole situation, other than my small supportive circle, was knowing the truth and not giving focus to what delusional views other people make up in their mind to make themselves feel better.

I have had to be patient with the police, their process, and try to remain positive that eventually he will leave me alone. I fully trust the Universe and my journey, and I believe there are positive ways to look at all setbacks in life.

The reason I have explained this story in detail to you is that I want to show you, even though we may encounter setbacks and negativity, it is us who holds the power in what we allow into our souls. We decide what can control us. We always have the choice to either focus on the negative or to focus on the positive. The worst I ever wish on people is that they meet themselves in someone else.

This situation could have completely destroyed me, but I have continued forward, towards my happiness and securely inside my thick glass tunnel.

MINDSET AND THOUGHTS

Be Aware, Observe ... But Don't Hold On

So far in this book we have touched on how substantial our thoughts, feelings, and mindsets really are. We are understanding how much of an impact they have, on a, our internal and external worlds, and b, how we are in control of what we choose to give focus to ... therefore we are in control of how we feel.

On average, we have around 70,000 thoughts per day, and that is just a normal person (an over-thinker like me has much more). That is roughly 4,300 PER HOUR ... if you sleep 8 hours a night that is. What is remarkably interesting, and quite worrying, is that of those 70,000 thoughts, a huge 75% of them are negative, and 95% of them are just repetitive. This constant flow of negative and 'auto-pilot' repetitive thoughts we have each day, can significantly impact our mental and physical health, our happiness, and our general wellbeing.

Repetitive thoughts are like a strong flowing river; they can become so deeply ingrained in our brains that it becomes difficult to break the cycle. This is why it is so important to become aware and make the necessary adjustments if you want to experience a happier and healthier, more successful life.

I once read that thoughts are just like trains at a train station. Imagine you are standing on the platform of a busy train station; there are multiple trains that go past you in which you can either choose to get on and ride for a while, or not. If you are on a train and you do not like where it is taking you, or if you do not believe this 'train of thought' is serving you, you can get off that train and onto another one, any time you like. A reminder however, the longer you do stay on the wrong train, the more expensive it is, and the longer it will take to go back home.

The most beneficial way that I have found to enhance the positive thoughts and to reduce the negative/anxious thoughts, is to simply observe the negative thoughts **and not hold on to them**. Ideally, not giving them any substance, meaning or attachment. This means you begin to see them from outside of the box, with an indifferent perspective. For example, if you are about to have a panic attack or your brain is telling you why you are not good enough, or why you can't do something, just detach from that initial thought. Do not give it any meaning or attachment and then let it dissolve and be on its way.

Maybe imagine this voice as an annoying Aunt Karen who doesn't believe you are good enough. She will try to tell you all of the reasons why you can't do something. All you need to do is just say, 'Thanks for your input, but not today Aunt Karen'. Then prove her wrong by doing it!

Positivity and Optimism

Ever wonder why positive and optimistic people seem to have it all? Everything seems to go their way, they have the dream relationship, and they never seem to get ill. That is because they are consciously aware of their thinking. They choose what they want to focus on every single day. They do not allow the negative media/friends/family/work colleagues/strangers/customers/newspapers to affect their internal being.

It not only feels amazing to be positive and optimistic, but it also has major physical health benefits. Studies have proven that people who have a positive and optimistic view on life have better heart health, a greater resistance to illnesses and even have a longer life span. A review of 15 studies, with over 200,000 participants, found a 35% lower chance of getting heart disease, and a 14% lower chance of early death in people who were optimistic. Optimistic people have better results following surgery, lower blood sugar and cholesterol, and have a higher immunity to infections and cancers.

If you can learn to change your behaviours and become more positive and optimistic, you will have a huge 50%

greater chance of living past 85 than people with a negative outlook! That is an incentive to change!

Your thoughts literally do create your life. They have created your past and they will create your future. So now is the time to make your thoughts work FOR you, and no longer AGAINST you. Worrying, self-imposed stress and anxiety are all in fact using your minds imagination against yourself. Confidence, curiosity, and optimism are all using your imagination to serve yourself. So, either one that you decide to choose, your mind will use it to shape your reality and will eventually convince you that it is truth.

You Can Choose How You React

From small day to day inconveniences, to life altering circumstances and everything in-between, you can actually choose how you react to everything. Every single situation and event are neutral until we give it any kind of meaning. It is our belief system that has created an opinion of it by attaching it to a previous similar situation, and then we choose to react to it (normally instantly and with no conscious thought). This is done through conditioning and past experiences and is basically an autopilot reaction.

Just say that a driver cuts you up in front, maybe your initial thought process would be to get angry, annoyed, and even want to start an argument with that person. Right in that very moment, you can decide how you want to react and if you want your autopilot reaction to take over, like it always has. You can decide if you are going to let the situation effect YOUR mood, YOUR energy, and YOUR day.

Do they deserve that satisfaction knowing that they have that ability and power over you to control how you think and feel? Which will more than likely put you in a negative mindset all morning.

What we could do in this situation is consciously choose to be compassionate and understanding towards the driver. They could be having the morning from hell. They could be on their way to see a parent that is about to pass away, their child could be in the emergency room, or they could have left the garage door open.

Whatever their reason might be, would it not feel better for you to just accept the situation, wish them well in your mind and reserve your energy? That way, you can carry on your morning with positive energy, and as a result, be completely un-effected by the person who cut you up. There is something very satisfying about harnessing this kind of control over your own reactions. It is where your power lies.

This will initially feel like using a new muscle at first, but the more you consciously do it, the easier it will become. You will be creating a new and more positive neural pathway for yourself.

'Never get upset by people or situations... both are powerless without your reaction' – *A teaching from buddha*

Now hear me out, I know you are probably thinking, 'Well how on earth can I choose to be happy at the fact I dropped the milk carton all over the kitchen floor, when I'm already half an hour late for work?' or 'How can I choose to be happy at the fact that I've suddenly become disabled and my whole world is now different?'.

OK, let's take the first scenario ... you are rushing around one busy morning, and you are running half an hour late for work. You make your coffee and grab your to-go cup, which annoyingly results in you spilling the entire milk carton all over the kitchen floor. You know that cleaning this up will set you back another 15 minutes, which will then probably make you miss the bus. You are now looking at potentially being over an hour late for work. I will give you one of the best pieces of advice, and a completely new way to look at this situation ... this will change your whole mindset when it comes to potential future 'obstructions' and being late.

In the Universe, there is no 'being late'. Everything is happening at exactly the right time. Precisely when it should. When something like this happens, and what may seem to be setting you back with your day, it is in fact, the complete opposite.

The Universe is always protecting you, and when a situation like this happens, it is potentially saving you from a negative event that you may have been involved in, had you left an hour before and were 'on time'. Your path could have crossed with some other person, which may have caused a fatal collision if you left when you had planned to. Something could have fallen in the street and hit you. Whatever it may be, this is exactly the time when you must be thankful, because like I said, the Universe always has your back.

Just say you lived in New Jersey and you started work every morning at 8:30am in The World Trade Center, New York. You are at your apartment, late for work and cleaning up that spilt milk. At 8:46am on September 11th, 2001, the North tower was hit by suicide attackers on an American Airline flight. Just imagine how many people called in sick or were running late that day because of spilt milk and will now see a slight inconvenience of running late or having the flu as such a huge blessing.

It is known that multiple famous figures missed the Titanic's voyage and therefore survived. There are many reasons why they didn't make the departure, some most famous reasons include missing the sail time due to illness, urgent business matters which required earlier travel on a different liner, and a sprained ankle. All of these situations at the time were most probably seen as an inconvenience and almost disappointing to the passengers that they were unable to sail on the famous Titanic.

Let's take the second scenario that I mentioned ... I am going to give you two stories of people who were struck with the unimaginable, and yet did not let the situation control them in a negative way. In fact, they both took their futures into their own hands, fought back, and made a success story out of their 'misfortune'.

Ryan Boyle is a perfect example proving that if you have a positive and motivated mindset, and work hard enough, you really can achieve anything. At the age of only nine years old, Ryan was hit and dragged by a pick-up truck which caused him to immediately go into a coma. Emergency brain surgery was performed on Ryan to save his life, but sadly he lost a portion of the back of his brain. At the age of just ten, he had to learn how to breathe, swallow, talk, eat, sit, walk ... everything.

When he was a freshman in high school, he wrote his own book called 'When the Lights Go Out: A Boy Given A Second Chance'. Since then, he went on to win gold, silver, and bronze medals in the World Championships for cycling, and won a silver medal in the Paralympics.

Melissa Stockwell was deployed to Iraq in 2004, she became the first female American soldier to lose a limb during combat. Her vehicle was hit by a roadside bomb which resulted in her losing her leg. When this happened to her, she made a promise to herself in that very moment that she would not allow this horrific experience to prevent her from living her life to the fullest.

Just 4 years after this tragic event, she became the first Iraq veteran to qualify for the Paralympics. In 2008 she competed in swimming at the Beijing Paralympics, where she was also selected to be the flag bearer for Team USA. She then turned to triathlon and went on to compete in the 2016 Paralympic games, where she became a bronze medallist and again in Tokyo 2021. She finished 5th in Paralympic triathlon in Paris, 2024.

There are so many motivational success stories similar to these two. They could have easily allowed their traumatic events to have a negative effect on their lives. They could have stayed in a victim 'Why me, this is not fair, I can't do anything with my life now' mindset, but what they did was the complete opposite.

When you realise that you are in control of how you respond to a situation, and it is you that has the choice of how you perceive it, you will then have a sense of understanding, compassion, freedom, and control.

Years ago, I was a Field Sales Representative for a media company. I would have to drive around to local car dealerships and garages to take care of their online and print advertising. One day, I was out on a customer visit at a local prestige car dealership. After the meeting, the owner walked me out of the office and down towards my car. He said to me, 'Sam, you always seem so positive and happy, no matter how many times we say no to your advertising', followed by

'Take care and don't get wet'. It was a beautiful warm summers day, so I asked him what he meant by this.

He explained that if you imagine all of life's negativities (people and thoughts) in a big swimming pool, and you are standing on the edge of the pool, dry, he said they will try to splash you and get you wet, just like them ... 'You need to keep moving, keep going and keep dodging them, so you don't get 'wet', he said.

You Are More Than Just the Voice in Your Head

In the book 'The Power of Now' written by Eckhart Tolle, he says, "Realising that you are not your thoughts is when you begin to awaken spiritually." Once you understand this, it will be lifechanging. Not only is this book so substantial in helping us understand that we are more than just our minds, but the book also helps us understand the real power of the present moment (We will discuss this together in the final chapter).

Every day, from as far back as we can remember, our lives have had a constant running commentary inside our mind. This voice thinks, helps us make decisions, analyses, learns, recalls memories, questions, and talks to us. Due to the fact that we are close to this voice, it is continuously there, and it even speaks in our own verbal voice, many people believe that this voice is what makes us, 'us' and that this voice is the 'Self'.

Try this, become aware of that voice right now. And become aware of your body right now. This is the real SELF ... the awareness of the thoughts and the awareness of the body. Our true 'Self' is actually the awareness. It is energy. It is, and will always be, moving and vibrating. We will talk about this in more detail later, but for now, understanding that we are the awareness of the thoughts and not the actual thoughts themselves, is crucial.

Psychologists call this ability to step back from the content of our thoughts 'cognitive defusion', which is considered a healthier and much more beneficial way of being. By understanding that the thoughts in our head are not who we are and are not the 'Self', we can use this information to our advantage. One major benefit of being aware of this knowledge is when the self-sabotage creeps in. When you have thoughts like, 'I'm a mess, I'm not good enough, I'm ugly' or 'I'm unimportant', know that this is the ego talking and not your true 'Self'. Our brain is only a tool, and we can decide to use it in a negative or positive way, through awareness.

Meditation is very much about bringing your awareness to your breath and your physical body, so the mind can be quiet and still. By repeatedly bringing our focus to our breath, and observing when our mind wanders, we naturally start to develop awareness of where our mind is and where it is going, from a detached perspective. The more we practice this during meditation and throughout the day, the more we will become familiar with being aware of our thoughts. We will begin to notice the detachment from the ego voice in our mind and see that we are the awareness. That will be the defining moment. The psychological benefit is profound. Life will still be happening, and things will still distract us, but when our default is to be aware of where our thoughts are, we are more balanced, psychologically healthier, and less at the mercy of them.

Not only is it important to be aware of our negative thoughts, mind, and internal feelings to be able to make the necessary changes, but it is also pivotal that we are conscious and aware of the words we are verbalising. We speak negatively about others but also about ourselves. And guess what? … you are always listening. Start to bring your awareness to how you speak about your Self and how you speak about the world around you. Many people verbalise things that are not truth and are even on autopilot due to self-sabotage and insecurities. You may say out loud to others the things about yourself that you are insecure about …just because you will feel better about getting it out into the open before they notice it about you. In actual fact, they more than likely were not even thinking about it.

By observing your own negative internal and external talk, you will be able to reduce the tendency of self-sabotage for one, but also you will then put a stop to negative manifesting and attracting. When you talk, speak, and think negatively, you are putting it out there to the Universe yourself ... and the Universe always listens and delivers. What we verbalise in our speech is a huge factor in what we manifest and bring into our reality. So be aware and mindful of your words. You may not realise that you may be the very reason you are experiencing more unwanted negativity in your life.

CONFIDENCE

Why It's Essential

I have decided to dedicate a whole chapter in this book for 'confidence' alone, and not just a sub section, due to its great significance. Confidence in oneself is crucial, not only for professional growth but also for one's personal growth. Gaining self-confidence enables us to trust ourselves enough to take the risks, to pursue bigger and better opportunities, to handle challenges and setbacks, and to achieve our goals ... all with greater resilience and success. Having true confidence within yourself and your own personal abilities is a huge part of what will elevate your life in all areas. Believing in yourself creates a thick-confident skin, which acts as a barrier to all of the negativity in the outside world, but it also protects the beautiful trust, vulnerability, 'knowing' and contentment within us.

Negative comments and situations may attempt to try and hurt us and want to pierce through us like arrows, but a thick invisible glass shield will deflect them back into the Universe. Achieving unwavering self-confidence and 'knowing' deep down within you that you are fully capable will bring self-assurance, trust in your Self, and build resilience to the outside world. You will be able to deal with any pressure you may face, you will make a strong and admirable impression to other people, and you will also be able to take action without any doubt.

The reason why obtaining confidence in yourself is so important is because by doing so, you will change for the better and you will never accept anything other than the very best. You will be able to negotiate much better career opportunities that may be offered to you, and you will be immune to any negativity you may be faced with from others (or yourself). This will propel you forward in your life, and it will give you a greater sense of personal empowerment. As a result, you will begin to see vast improvements in all areas. Your romantic relationships and connections will improve. Your professional career will be enhanced. You will start wanting to learn more skills, and actively seek out new knowledge and education. All to enhance your Self and mind.

The mere thought of failing will no longer prevent and scare you from 'putting yourself out there' and exposing yourself. If you are struggling with self-confidence right now, do not panic, we can begin to change that right now, but first, let's get clear in our minds on the difference between self-confidence and egotistical arrogance.

The Right Kinda Confidence

Let's not get it twisted, I am not advising you to become egotistic or arrogant. That is ugly and unnecessary ... detrimental even. It pushes people away, both within your support circle and potential professionals that could pull you up to the level you wish to be at. What I am talking about is pure, unwavering, internal Self confidence. Confidence is completely different from arrogance. It is not about trying to feel a shallow sense of superior to others by bringing them down, only to feel as though you are lifting yourself up, but rather about having a realistic and true sense of your own personal capabilities. Staying in your lane, if you like.

Self-confidence has so many benefits, it leads to improved self-esteem, it builds stronger communications with others, and most of all it results in greater resilience to setbacks that are out of our hands. This ultimately contributes to a better quality of life, helps us build life purpose and increases our overall success.

Being arrogant and egotistic is what people tend to portray only when they LACK true self-confidence. Ironic, isn't it? Whilst traits like arrogance and egotism stem from a sense of self-importance, which in itself is great, it can be self-destructive and counterproductive. By having these traits, it can lead to really poor decision making. Due to the fact that all opinions will be viewed from a selfish, insecure and narrow-minded perspective. It can damage both personal and professional relationships. Not to mention it gives a serious lack of self-awareness and humility. AKA ugly.

A false, inflated sense of Self makes people resistant and scared to receive valuable feedback. They are unwilling to consider alternative, more beneficial perspectives. This unfortunately means zero growth for them. It means losing out on decent relationships, people that can propel you forward, and potentially, huge business progression. You will notice that arrogant characters will often struggle to accept or take on board any constructive criticism, viewing it only as a personal attack, rather than a great opportunity for growth.

Constructive criticism, to me, has immeasurable value. I always savour the opportunity for growth and learning. Because that is exactly what constructive criticism is, an opportunity for growth. It should, however, only be accepted when it is an opinion from someone who is above you and doing BETTER in that particular area.

You will probably start to realise two things; that criticism and negative hate speech usually comes from the people that are below you, and constructive criticism that can be of benefit to you will only come from people that are above you. Someone with self-confidence will take and accept constructive criticism with both hands, dissect it, evaluate it … and then implement it into their lives. Knowing that they will achieve a new valued, priceless, step towards their own greatness. People with fake, shallow confidence will shut off constructive criticism completely. They will take it as a personal attack that they are not good enough. They will never be self-aware and allow the personal growth advice from others, due to the fact that it will seem beneath them. This is a false mindset that they have wired within their brain that makes them feel superior to others.

True self-confidence is strong, unwavering, empowering and grounding. It comes from knowing your strengths and recognising your achievements. No one can take true self-confidence away from you. No matter how many setbacks, negative words, or negative criticism you are hit with. The wrong kind of confidence is weak, shallow, unstable and comes only from a place of internal insecurities. This kind will always prevent true love, personal growth, and valued, secure success. Your confidence needs to be built from within. If you build confidence on compliments, it will always shatter with criticism.

Rewind and Rewire!

OK, so in order to gain and maintain true self-confidence at an adult age, if you have not already done so, is to rewind it right back. Rewind your mind to exactly where the insecurity first originated. Then, dissect the scenario. Understand where the insecurities came from and start to rewire a new, beneficial reality.

Let's first begin with the big question ... why are you like this? Sit with this question for a little while and start to dig deep. What was the actual cause that resulted in you feeling insecure and have a lack of confidence with this particular situation? The answer might take a few minutes, or even a few days to come to the surface and be fully noticeable, but what is important to know is that you will eventually get to the real reason behind it. This is key in dissolving all insecurities.

It may be the case that someone once verbalised a negative comment to you years ago when you felt vulnerable at the time, and it happened to stick with you ever since. It may be that a parent put you down, or they had a certain quote or phrase that they would say repeatedly when you were a child, which therefore soaked into your subconscious. Maybe, you did something that you spent loads of time and effort on and were completely proud of, only to be shot down and told it was not good enough.

Whatever it may be, getting to the exact root and understanding why you currently believe that to be truth, is essential. This is the only way to begin the process of dissolving the issue so you can move forward, with confidence.

When you understand where the insecurities originated, we have to then question two things. Firstly, was what was said about you actually the truth? Secondly, did it come from someone higher and more advanced than you in that department? It is important to now start removing any emotional attachment to this scenario and question was this a truthful and factual opinion?

Once you step outside of the box and evaluate this situation from a non-emotional viewpoint, you will be able to clearly see if this was a valid point given from the other person. Were they doing better than you? What position were they in personally? Could it have been jealousy? Did they feel intimidated by you at the time? Was this the only way for them to feel protected themselves?

Lastly, once you have evaluated all of these things, the final question is this ... Do you feel like you WANT to change it? If someone made a negative comment on your appearance, maybe they slammed you for your lack of knowledge on a subject or put you down for hundreds of other reasons. Ask your Self, do you really want to improve and change that part of you?

Of course, changing ourselves for anyone other reason other than because WE desire to, is not the right reason to make any changes. Plus, long lasting changed for this reason will be short lived and unattainable. However, if the change is because you want it, and it's to improve your future, then that is a completely different story entirely.

Once you evaluate where the insecurity issue came from, remove the emotional attachment, see who put that belief into your head, and determine whether or not it was constructive criticism, or just straight up slamming ... you can come to the conclusion whether or not this is a potential change that will benefit you moving forward.

If you do want to improve your appearance, expand your knowledge, or gain the materialistic items around you, then go for it, but only do so because YOU see the benefits.

If you reach the decision that in actual fact, you do not need to change a damn thing, and the problem is not because of how you look or your capabilities at all, then it is likely that you would have come to the conclusion that the issue was always with them, not you. That is the eureka moment that will unlock you.

Unfortunately arrogant, egotistic, and insecure people are more than happy to put others down for no true, valid reason, other than to feed their own insecurities and attempt to temporarily lift themselves up. People will dislike you for being confident about the very things that they are insecure about.

After doing these steps and breaking your old deep-rooted beliefs down, you can then start to rewire your brain and create new neural pathways with your more confident reality. Conscious thinking, positive reinforcement, and time, will collectively begin to dissolve the old unwanted past and create this new productive reality.

Start bringing your focus to your personal strengths and why you are so unique and special. Look back at previous achievements that you have accomplished and focus on all of the areas where you have been successful. Savour those moments and memories. Positively dwell on them. Re-live them in your mind vividly and remember the feelings you experienced. Start to take care of your physical and mental health if you don't already. Seek new learning and education if necessary. Start replacing your negative self-talk to positive self-talk every time you catch yourself going down that downward spiral.

Start setting new goals, big or small, and achieve them so you can prove to your Self that you ARE capable. Do the thing that you have always put off or been too scared to start. Show your Self that you can. Make the people who put you down initially swallow and regret their words with your new reality. Be around the people who lift you up, the people who motivate you and the people who admire you.

If there happens to be a negative comment about you online, good, start to get into the habit of swiping, deleting, and blocking. Not allowing it to seep into your being. No one has time for that kind of negativity. Even start to do this in person, swipe delete and block people in real life if they try to belittle you or make you feel worthless constantly.

Bye-bye.

This will take some conscious thinking of course; you are probably unpicking multiple years of deep-rooted insecurities that your subconscious mind believes to be truth. But understand that your brain put it there … and your brain can also remove it. That will only happen with creating new, conscious habits moving forward. Every time a negative, insecure or self-doubt thought comes into your head, stop it in its tracks and tell it, no! That is not the truth, I used to believe that but now I understand that it does not serve me anymore.

New Self Assurance

By doing everything we have just discussed, you will be building a new story of solid, self-confidence and self-assurance, that no one will be able to take away from you. Working on this is so transformative and life changing. You will start to have more trust in your Self. You will be open to so many new opportunities. When you have re-wired your old insecure beliefs to the new, confident beliefs, you would have successfully created such a rooted existence that you will never need any validation from others.

That is a completely liberating and uplifting feeling. You will be free from the negative comments and the negative people that try to put you down, because you will have a new sense of KNOWING, and TRUSTING, in your Self. The only person that you need to compare yourself to, impress, or be better than, is yourself. When you work through and heal from your past, when you remove everything that you do not want in your present life, and when you begin to see the amazing results from manifesting everything that you do want, you will gain and begin to ooze so much self-confidence as a result. When the internal is finally in alignment, that is when your confidence will radiate.

We are all human and no one is perfect. Trust in your abilities, stay in your lane and know deep down that you are fully capable. Change for the better only if YOU want to.

This is now your new story. The past is no more, and it can no longer harm you, prevent you from doing things or pull you down. If anyone tells you that you can't, do it twice and take a damn photo I say!

LAW OF ATTRACTION

What It Is

I am sure, given that you have this book in your hands right now, that you already have an idea of what the Law of Attraction is all about. It's what many self-help writers and speakers start with. The Law of Attraction is a Universal Law that states that we attract everything into our lives, stemming from our thoughts and feelings. We are all vibrational magnets that manifest everything that is currently in our lives, and everything that will eventually come into our lives ... both good and bad. Whether we are conscious of this Law or not.

When I first heard about the Law of Attraction, I thought it was for wishful thinkers and people that were unrealistic. As that was my mindset at the time, and because I believed that to be true, my life was continuously negative. I was attracting things like ill mental health, terrible physical health and negative relationships. I felt a constant dark cloud above my head. Victim mentality if you like.

Once I came around to the idea that we really do have the ability to create and manifest anything that we wish, I thought I would experiment with it to see if I could test the 'theory' out on my own life .... that is when my life dramatically changed for the better.

Human beings tend to have an, 'I will believe it when I see it' kind of mentality. And I can fully understand that mindset. However, when I think about it, I don't understand how electricity works, I don't understand how aeroplanes function and stay up in the air, I don't understand how gravity keeps us standing up ... but I do know that all of these particular Laws DO work, and we all benefit from them every single day.

The Law of Attraction is ALWAYS happening, whether you know about it or not, and whether you believe in it or not. The Law of Attraction is a vibrational Law, and as you know, we are all energy beings, so, the vibrations that we are admitting outwards are exactly what we will be attracting. How we think and how we feel is exactly what we will continuously attract through The Law of Attraction. Throughout. Our. Entire. Lives. Understanding, accepting, and applying this Law into your life, believer or not, will make you see that you can begin to use it to your advantage.

How to Use It

In earlier chapters, we have discussed how crucial being aware of our thoughts and feelings is, how important it is to adjust them to be in line with how we want to feel and, as a result, attract what we want to attract. Although thoughts and feelings are both major keys in using the Law of Attraction to advance and benefit your life, unfortunately it doesn't just stop there. You would be surprised to know just how many books that I have read in the past that simply say, 'Think about what you want', 'Feel as though it is already yours', 'Write out your positive affirmations 2000 times each day' ... and then hey presto, it's yours. These are all true and certainly do help massively with the process, **but there are vital components missing for an effective formula.** There are **four key elements** that need to be applied if you want to become a master at working with the Law of Attraction;

1, BE SPECIFIC AND DETAILED ON WHAT IT IS THAT YOU WANT TO ATTRACT

What career is it that you want to be in? What kind of partner do you want? What physical and mental health do you wish for yourself? What spiritual journey do you want in this lifetime? What materialistic items do you want to gain around you?

Then start to get specific and detailed with those desires. How will it feel internally when you achieve that position? What will the sense of pride, success, and freedom feel like?

How will that perfect partner make you feel on a day-to-day basis? How will getting ready for that date night with them feel? What will it feel like to prepare their food and get their things ready for them to start their day? Imagine the feeling of recovering from your old toxic relationship and finding someone who treats you right.

What will you be able to do when you finally become mentally and physically stable again? Where will you go? What will you plan to see and experience? How will you feel when you start to practice spiritualism each day? Will you feel more connected to the planet and in-tune with the Universe?

When you have attracted the forever home, what materialistic items will you have around you, and how will it feel to enjoy them with your loved ones?

If you are struggling with deciding what it is that you really want in life, there was a question I was once asked which was, 'What would you want to do with your life if you had all of the money in the world?'. Without consciously thinking, my automatic reaction inside of me was that I wanted to help people through writing. I had an unwavering feeling of wanting to make people happy again. To help traumatised people move on from their past, to help people remove the toxic negativity in their current lives which is holding them back, and to show people a way to reach the life they truly desire and deserve.

That is such a great question ... 'What would you want to do with your life if you had all of the money in the world?'. This question opens our mind and makes us aware of what our true feelings and wants are, if the stress and pressure of attaining money was unimportant. Sit with this question for a while and make some notes with whatever comes into your mind.

Once you know exactly what it is that you want, you then have to do the following in order to make the Law of Attraction work for you –

2, THINK ABOUT IT CONSTANTLY UNTIL IT IS YOURS (By doing this, it will naturally get you feeling good, excited, and positive ... therefore you will be kickstarting the attraction by sending out the specific vibrations to the universe)

3, MAKE ROOM FOR IT (Like we discussed before, you must allow both physical and mental room for what it is that you desire. For example, build the courage to end the relationship with the partner that doesn't feed your soul, or clear out a cupboard to store new treats, food, and water bowls for your new puppy)

4, **TAKE ACTION** (You will have to actively make moves to reach your goal, for example, updating and sending out your CV with a cover letter explaining why they need you in their business, researching a new location in the world to potentially move to, or arranging dinner and drinks with a friend in a place that you believe a potential new partner would also go to).

That is literally it. It is not complicated or really hard to do. The process will be easy for you if the strong desire is there, and it falls in line with your morals and values.

There is one part which we have just discussed that people always skip ... many people miss out the **taking action** part, and just believe that they can think things into existence. That is when you get the non-believers who think you are crazy and that, 'No one can simply think about a brand-new Mercedes and miraculously have one turn up at their door with a big red bow on it the next day'. They are the people who are straight up disappointed because, 'It didn't work'. This is because these people don't **take the action** to reach their goals, and yet, they still expect the results. They didn't align with their desire.

Aligned action is required for you to manifest the life that you truly want. Take the steps by making the room for your desire and put yourself in the position that will give you the best opportunities. You do not need to know HOW your desire will eventually manifest into existence, that is for the Universe to take care of. Simply by doing your part and meeting the Universe halfway, trust me, it will definitely take care of the rest for you.

The Art of Being Patient

OK, I get it, when we desire something, we can sometimes get impatient and frustrated because we want it right this second. We can feel as though we are lacking in our current circumstances, and so, dwell on the fact that we have not already manifested what we want. I am here to say to you that if you implement all of the steps in this book, you will undoubtedly get what it is that you desire ... you may just have to wait for the Universe to deliver it to you at the correct time.

Trust me when I say, if it is genuinely what you truly want and deserve, it will eventually manifest into your reality and it will most certainly be worth the wait. Hearing this may initially sound fairly disheartening, however, what you need to understand is that there is so much beauty in 'the waiting' part.

Once you begin to fully trust in the process, you will start to admire the Universe's work and understand its perfect timing. As we now know, timing is so crucial. Everything happens to you at exactly the right time that it is meant to. Nothing can be rushed or forced. This is the time to relish in the beauty of being patient.

There are normally two scenarios when it comes to The Law of Attraction; you may be given an opportunity in life, whether that be a new partner or a new promotion at work, that wasn't even on your radar. Something that feels completely out of the blue. This is when you run with the experience, headfirst, and it turns out to be the best thing that has ever happened to you. Or, on the flip side, you may have desired and tried to manifest something in particular for such a long time, yet it still has not materialised into your life … continuously remaining almost impossible to reach, no matter how hard you have previously tried. When the latter happens, it really is because there is some internal growth and evolution within you that needs to happen first. This process needs to take place in order for you to be fully ready to receive what it is that you want. This could include some kind of therapy and/or counselling sessions that you may need so that you can work on, and process, the past traumatic events you have experienced. It could even be crucial characteristic development that may be essential for you to reach and master before you will be truly ready for that next stage in your life. Both of which are key for you to be able to not only obtain the desired want but also maintain and secure it for the long term.

Just one personal example I have of experiencing this is when I met my fiancé. From the ages of 16 to 28 I had been treated with little to no respect from men in romantic relationships … so I decided to protect myself and be single, get happy and soak up the valuable experience. And that is exactly what I did.

I lived by myself in a beautiful little home just off the seafront. I started a new online lingerie business that I had always dreamt of owning since I was 16. I focused more on modelling and meeting new photography friends. I read so many self-help books and delved deeper into improving my mental health. I painted and spent time drawing to focus my mind. I walked on the beach daily to process and clear my unwanted thoughts. I got my dachshund, Leo, which I had been manifesting for years.

I was happy and content in my own skin and the little bubble that I had created. I knew deep down that I did not need another human being to fulfil me or to make me feel as though I was 'complete', I already was. I began to take care of myself for the first time, and I made a promise to myself that I would remain that way until someone completely amazing were to come along, if ever. I did exactly that. I stopped actively looking for a romantic relationship until it was just no longer on my radar or in my conscious mind.

Instead, I decided to do even more internal work through reading and research. Let's face it, if you want to attract a decent human being who treats you right and be able to actually hold on to them, you need them to have something decent to hold on to as well, right?

I completed an online Life Coaching course, I bought books on deep-rooted negative belief systems and how to rewire them, I started to point the finger at myself and question why I was treated so badly in the past. One of the many realisations that I had was that I was a huge factor in the problem. With this knowledge however, I knew that I was also the solution and the change that I so desperately needed in order to sustain a long, committed, and loyal relationship in the future.

Once I mentally and emotionally made room for a true love that I had always deserved, you guessed it, I received it. The internal work had been done, and the timing was finally right. Andy is like no other man that I have ever met before. The love and support he gives me on a daily basis is unwavering and pure. He is so beautifully patient with me, even when I'm not patient with myself. Especially in the beginning when I had a lot of internal work to do on my own insecurities and trust issues, which I was bringing into the relationship from previous. He is so committed to our relationship and future. So respectful of my feelings, emotions, and views. A love that I will forever soak up, savour, and be grateful for.

I fully believe, and now luckily understand, why I was never ready to receive this relationship before. I had to use the 'art of being patient' in order to receive the love and commitment I now do from Andy. Just say that he had come into my life any time previously, the timing would have set the relationship up to fail.

Without the knowledge I have now, I would have pushed him and the relationship away due to the 'self-preservation' mindset I used to have. Thinking I was protecting myself from being hurt, and therefore, doing myself a favour. When in fact, the only way I could have become this happy in a relationship was for me to spend the time doing the internal work on myself.

I needed to learn and understand that just because I have never trusted anyone in my life previously, it does not mean that I could not trust the right person in the future. I needed to learn and understand that just because my parents went through a divorce when I was young, it does not mean that all marriages will break down and end that way. I needed to learn and understand how to be patient when it comes to nurturing and growing a new relationship. How to properly listen to understand, and not just listen to reply, which so many people do on autopilot. Also, I had to learn and understand how to be more empathetic towards him and his view, because this was something I really struggled with after living by myself and being single for so long. Of course, we have times where we need to air our views and opinions to each other to make sure the relationship stays healthy and strong. We can't avoid negative patches in relationships, however, we can learn to communicate, be understanding and grow together with that person.

Writing this book for you is another perfect example of a time where I've had to use the art of being patient. Many times, I would fire up the laptop (previous notes at hand, which I had written to make sure I include them), and I would be in complete flow with writing. Pages after pages would be written in just one sitting. I would have so much to tell you and explain that I would eventually look up at the time and hours would have gone by. Other times, I would stare blankly at my laptop screen, not knowing what to type.

I experienced a roadblock many times when I attempted to write and fill these pages for you. Those days of not knowing what to write made me feel disappointed, unproductive, and like a failure to be honest. That is exactly when I had to learn to be patient with myself and not to force the process.

I remember when this happened for not just one or two days, but for an entire month. The block on writing was beginning to make me feel low and as though the book would never be complete. Luckily, it came up in discussion at my reiki healing session. My healer Jenny said to me whilst I was on the table that I needed to learn to be patient with myself and trust the Universe. She explained that there is always a reason behind the delays and roadblocks and that in actual fact, there were reasons why the book writing came to a hold. She said there were certain situations and experiences that I had to go through so I would be able to include them in this book for you.

She was definitely correct, and you will find out why nearer the end of this book. Timing is everything and mastering the art of being patient is … absolutely priceless.

Trust

Having the ability to drop your guard, feel vulnerable and put your full trust into anything, whether it be with a person, a specific outcome, or a situation, can be the toughest act to do ... especially if your trust has been betrayed or damaged in the past. Once someone or something has breached your trust, it causes significant emotional distress and a serious lack of faith as a result.

It can take years to build up a level of trust, and sadly, it can take only seconds to destroy. This means that trusting that the Universe has always got your back, believing that it will only give you what you are capable of handling, and understanding that it will eventually give you everything that was meant for you and your journey ... may seem impossible.

I have been lied to, I have been cheated on, I have been let down and I have been left out in the cold. So, I am with you. I understand just how difficult it can be to even begin to try and trust anything again. I have been hurt and betrayed by the people that I loved unconditionally. I have been lied to and let down by family members that I believed would always be there for me. I have not had the outcome I wanted in situations, and as a result, instantly thought to myself that I have been screwed over by the Universe .... believing that all of my hard Law of Attraction manifesting was a complete waste of time.

It is not until after the event, and a certain amount of time has passed, that you can look back and actually be grateful for those things not manifesting. Grateful for the relationship that did not work out which would have left you destroyed and heartbroken. Grateful that you didn't get that certain job that you really wanted. By not receiving these things, it has helped shape you. By NOT obtaining them, it will eventually guide you to what is really meant for you.

When you change your perception of these situations you will understand and trust that they really are blessings in disguise. What these experiences do is give you a temporary guard, and a necessary layer of protection, until you reach the next, more beautiful, stage of your life.

Building emotional/mental barriers and walls around you is not always a negative thing, if seen and used in the correct way. They do help protect you and your emotional wellbeing as well as guide you at the time, however, if left for a long period of time after the event and not eventually addressed, that is when the problems can arise. Like I said, I have had to survive in my darkest days and the only way I was able to do that at the time was to build these walls and protect myself. I did that for years. I had no choice, as I am sure you didn't. But now we do have the choice ... only when we are fully aware, ready for the change, and when the time is right.

What I eventually came to realise was that being guarded and not trusting anyone for too long was just not healthy or beneficial. As my deep-rooted lack of trust was so imbedded and prominent in my life, I realised I was only holding myself back from moving forward. I was the one preventing the good coming into my life. Not anyone else who had betrayed me in the past. Me. Also, when I stepped back and evaluated how it felt not trusting anyone or anything, from a non-attached perspective, I came to the realisation that in actual fact, it honestly just felt terrible.

We know that we are the only ones who are in charge of how we think and therefore how we feel, so this was something I knew that I did have the ability and control to change. We need to rewire our brains and understand that just because people have hurt us in the past, it does not mean that other people will treat us the same way in the future.

We can even take it a step further and actually start being **thankful** to the people in the past that have wronged us, because they have shown us how we should NOT be treated, and what it is that we do not want. This is equally as important. Yes, the Universe brought them into our lives, but the Universe also removed them from our lives and left them in the past. Once we look back and see the **reason why** the person or situation came into our lives, we can begin to forgive them, **but not forget the lesson they taught us**.

Building up trust again will take some time, and a lot of patience from yourself and others around you. In the beginning you may feel overwhelming feelings of vulnerability and an uncomfortable 'openness'. If you are anything like me, you will want to get away.

What is important is that with this past experience, you will know deep down who truly deserves your trust and who does not. Hindsight is twenty-twenty and even if we have to take years of pain to get there, it still has huge advantages. Do not sleep on this knowledge you have taken years to gain.

The process will have its difficulties, like many things we have been discussing, so you will need to be patient and keep in mind why you have made the decision to work on this. Try to keep your focus on what the benefits of trusting again will eventually have for you.

Trusting again allows so many beautiful opportunities to come your way. Trusting again makes you open to endless possibilities. Not trusting means that you are preventing new potential and greatness coming into your life.

Trusting reminds me of playing the lottery. You must have a ticket to be in with a chance of winning the jackpot. Without a ticket, you will never win. Trusting in the Universe is necessary, and once you eventually achieve this level of trust, it will bring so much calm and tranquillity into your life and being. When you gain a deep-rooted knowing that whatever comes and goes in your life is always meant to be that way, you will dissolve any kind of unhealthy attachment, and gain full acceptance. This leaves a calming sense of reassurance, knowing that all outcomes will always be your true destiny.

Trusting in the Law of Attraction is exactly the same. Whatever it is that you truly desire and want to manifest, it will come to you. It just may not come in the form that you once believed it should. If you didn't get the job that you were trying so hard to manifest, it is because something bigger and better is meant for you. If you were wronged by that partner that you so badly desired, it is because you needed to grow, develop as an individual, and prepare yourself to love and to be open to be loved by the perfect partner in the future.

I have thankfully rewired my brain and gained full trust in The Law of Attraction, the Universe and whatever my journey shall bring. It took time and a lot of conscious effort along the way, but I know that moving forward anything negative in my life should be viewed as a lesson and an opportunity. An opportunity to a, work on something that I am clearly lacking internally, and b, an opportunity to be thankful, patient, and strengthen my trust that something bigger and better is meant for me. I believe that we are all destined for greatness.

Once we let go, fully trust, and ride the wave **with** the Universe, **instead of going against it,** and feeling like the victim, magnificence unfolds.

MANIFEST WHAT YOU WANT

Goals and Dreams - Get Clear

For you to be able to manifest the perfect life for yourself, like we discussed before, first you must get fully clear in your mind what your goals and dreams truly are. That seems pretty obvious though, right? But so many people only focus and fully know what it is that they DON'T want.

Why is it so easy for us to be really specific on what it is that we don't want? Why is it so easy for us to focus on all of the negative things? Our hang ups? Or the criticism we have been told about ourselves? Some people focus on and believe the negative things said about them so much more than any compliments they have ever received. When we change our thoughts and our focus to the positives instead of the negatives, we can then get clear on the things that we DO want to manifest.

Specifics are absolutely key with this, so instead of simply saying that you do not want to live where you are currently living because of X,Y and Z, start thinking about where you DO want to live. Then, get really precise … to the fine details.

If you want to manifest a beautiful home abroad, start describing what the house will look like. Will it be located on a lake? What will your perfect dog walk route near your house look like? How many rooms does the home have? What will you use some of the rooms for? Will there be an area for friends and family to vacate and stay with you? What will the garden space look like? Will there be a pool? Will there be garden furniture on a stone patio for you to sit and enjoy cheese and wine, whilst watching the sunset with your partner? As you can see, by being specific with what it is that you do want to manifest, you begin to attract a better and clearer visual in your mind's eye. This is what will accelerate the manifesting process.

Ask yourself, right now, what are my life goals and dreams? What is it that you want to achieve career wise? What legacy do you want to leave behind you? When you are taking your final breaths in this life, what would it be that made you feel satisfied that you managed to accomplish during your life? The more detailed and specific you can be about your life goals and dreams, the easier it will be to accomplish them and make it your reality.

Have you ever heard of the 'Red Car Theory'? The Red Car Theory explains that once you start focusing on something specific, you will start noticing it more and more frequently. This isn't because that thing has suddenly become more prevalent, but simply because your awareness has shifted on to it. Once you start getting clear on what your life goals and dreams are, and their specifics, you will be able to focus your mind on these outcomes, and therefore the manifestation process and the realisation of them will become easier.

What's Your Calling?

Like I briefly mentioned in a previous chapter, someone once asked me what I would want to do with my life if I had all of the money in the world. This is a great question when thinking about what your calling is. Your calling in life is something that you are good at, but also something that you feel passionate about. Passion is what propels us and motivates us to pursue our calling, and once we grow to become a master at doing it well, it is the sense of competence that continues to fuel the passion ongoing. It is a feeling of just 'knowing' that you were meant to do that particular thing.

To be able to find your calling in life is really a journey of Self-discovery and looking inwards. It involves exploring your passions, what gets you excited, and what's in line with your values and skills. Then aligning them all together with the actual activities that bring you feelings of purpose and fulfilment. What genuinely excites you and can make you completely lose track of time? What do you feel enthusiastic about when talking to someone? That is a profound way to start exploring what your calling is if you are unsure. What principles are most important to you in life? How do you want to live your life? What are you good at? What do you value? What do people compliment you on?

When you have a good idea of all the answers to these questions, it is time to start being in alignment with them. If you need to take some more courses to gain some extra knowledge on the subject, get it booked. Get ready to put yourself out there, attend the workshops and the seminars. Do the online courses. Travel where you need to go to make it happen. Get to know the people that inspire you and question them on absolutely everything.

When you discover what your calling in life is, you will experience a profound sense of internal purpose, motivation, and excitement. Your actions will start to match your plans. You will reach a state of 'flow' and you won't be easily distracted. What is more is that you will be happy throughout the journey and the process, not just once you have reached the destination.

Receiving Can Feel Uncomfortable ...

So, now you have started to receive everything that you have ever longed for, and your manifestations are now becoming your reality ... so why on earth does it feel this uncomfortable?? I thought it was meant to feel 100% amazing, all of the time?? I have said it myself and I can hear you saying it too, so let's talk about it.

When you begin to receive what you have been trying to manifest through the Law of Attraction, for the majority of the time you will feel content, happy, and 'in flow'. However, sometimes you may also feel things like pressure, self-doubt, isolation, and feelings of negativity. Now this does not mean that this person or situation is not meant for you, it is simply because you are now levelling up in your life.

Comfort zones are great, let's face it, they are comfortable right? But unfortunately, nothing ever amazing will happen to you if you continue to set up camp in your comfort zone for too long. Expanding to a new level in your life, in any area, means that you are now growing and moving from that previous smaller comfort zone. Which can be uncomfortable and uneasy at first.

Although you have longed for what you have now manifested, and you previously believed that it would make you feel incredible straight from the start, you will probably feel shocked by how you feel during this transitional period. Trust me when I say that this should not make you feel disheartened or believe that this was not meant for you. Starting a new career, moving to a new country, or beginning a new committed relationship are all beautiful things to experience in this life, however, if this is unknown territory for you, it can feel overwhelming sometimes. This is where we will need to begin to adapt.

An important factor to take note during these potentially bumpy times, is how it makes you feel **the majority of the time**. It is essential to keep being aware of your gut, your heart, and your mental health **on a whole,** to determine if this is truly what you desire, and if this is just a natural feeling of being uncomfortable due to the growth and expansion happening. Or, in some circumstances, this genuinely is not for you. You know your Self better than anyone on this planet, so only you will truly know the answer to what it is that you desire, and if you are in alignment with it. When you are completely honest and true with yourself, you will get the answers that you need.

I have been face to face with these uneasy and uncomfortable emotions a few times since moving here to Las Vegas from England. I adored Worthing, the seaside walks and my little home. Just me and my dachshund. I was wonderfully comfortable, don't get me wrong, but I just always knew deep down that some things were missing, and I still felt internally unfulfilled. Pushing myself out of my comfort zone to finally pack up my entire world to leave the country was a hugely vulnerable step for me. However, I knew deep down that this was the essential next stage in my life, and I fully trusted in the process. Even during the uncomfortable stages.

Since being here, I am not going to lie to you and say it has been easy all of the time. Of course, there have been some tough days, but they are trumped by all of the incredible days. The transition has certainly tested me emotionally, multiple times, but the growth has been beautiful. I have learnt so much about myself, expanded my mindset and been able to nurture and grow a precious relationship. All of which are of immeasurable value to me. Without firstly doing the internal work, secondly changing my old belief system, and lastly expanding my horizons, I would not have grown mind and soul to experience the blissful life that I live now.

Once you have understood within your Self that this really is your goal and your true desire, you can rest assure that although there may be slight turbulence and tough times along the way, the outcome will be beautiful. It could take six months to a year ... or even longer, depending on what kind of growth you are having to experience. Eventually though, the energies will level off and you will then feel pleasure, safety, contentment, and fulfilment. All of the feelings you knew you were meant to feel.

This is where even more magic and successful manifesting will begin to happen for you. You will be in a place where you can now attract and manifest even more that what you already have. Reach higher levels and forever expand. You will begin to fully trust the process. You will be trusting in the Law of Attraction and the Universe. You will have the feeling of **knowing** that this is your path and your true destiny. Only good will ever come from this magical level.

Always Expect It!!

One of the best habits that you can start getting into right now is ALWAYS expect the very best possible scenario, in every situation that you face. This can be labelled as being an optimist, but it is so much more than that. You will notice that the top tier manifestors in this world literally always expect the perfect outcome, in any circumstance. What is more is that not only do they foresee the ideal result, but their mindset will also go one step further than that. They believe that possibilities are endless for them, and they could potentially gain an even better result than what their current thoughts could even comprehend. They are always open to the idea, and the potentiality that something not even on their radar could occur. Just because they cannot see this potential result, it does not stop them from believing that it is possible.

By **knowing** it is already yours and **expecting** it each and every time, you are telling the Universe **that it is yours, you are ready and that you deserve it.** This is such a powerful force because you will start to become a magnet to every amazing opportunity available to you. Let's face it, the internal feeling of knowing you will always get the very best outcome, or more so, feels so much better than always expecting the worst. When you expect the worst in everything, it feels dreadful, and it sets you up to attract failure before you have even started.

It is a proven fact that many world-renowned athletes continuously play out their winning performances mentally in their head before the event actually happens. They see themselves winning in their mind, repeatedly. To them, doing this visualisation is equally as important as physically practicing the sport itself.

When you start making this thought choice a regular habit, it will create a new neural pathway in your brain so that with any situation moving forward, it will become easier to always expect the best possible outcome. You could be waiting on a call regarding a promotion at work, you could be preparing for a speech you have to make, you could be planning a date with a potential partner ... it could be anything! A car space, an exam, a fresh batch of warm bread at the bakery at exactly the time that you arrive – any scenario, no matter how big or small.

Not only does 'expecting it' make you feel more positive and optimistic, the ongoing habit and behaviour will help expand your mindset to the unlimited potential of bigger and better things ... which in turn will actually help you attract more opportunities!

I remember when I was in my early twenties, and I went to Marbella, Spain to dance as a stripper for a few weeks with a girl friend. This was the trip that the fellow stripper friend introduced me to the book The Secret by Rhonda Byrne, The Law of Attraction and the idea of manifesting positive outcomes.

There was one evening we went to work at this particular club and before the venue opened, the dancer was talking out loud saying, 'Tonight will be the night a group of rich and respectful men will walk in and spend so much money on all of us'. I will never forget the instant feeling and opinion I had on her view. I thought, at the time, that she was delusional because the club had been so quiet. Hardly any customers were coming in, let alone spending loads of money in there! I responded saying something along the lines of, 'Well you are living in cloud cuckoo land, that is just never going to happen' ... whilst eye-rolling, I'm sure.

When she explained that she was an optimist, I replied by saying, 'Yeh well, I'm a realist' ... Honestly, I cringe to this day at that memory and my narrow mind. Luckily, throughout the next few weeks on the trip she schooled me and helped me to open my eyes. Which was actually the major turning point in my life that I am forever grateful for.

That was roughly fifteen years ago now and I would like to say that with everything I have learnt, changed, and implemented in my life, I am always expecting the very best outcomes now. So much so that friends, family, and strangers radiate to me specifically because of that mindset I now have. They reach out and want to hear my views and opinions on situations they are going through because they need to hear an alternative, more optimistic view that they may be struggling to see. You will start to become 'that person'. The person that good results happen to. The one that always gets the good deal, or things just turn out well for. Some might even call you 'jammy'. This will become noticeable in your energy too, not just by the positive results surrounding you.

When others notice this change in you, they will want to know your secret. They will be asking you for advice and valuing your responses. They will be copying you and following in your footsteps. Imitation is the best form of flattery, right? So, help them! Spread this knowledge! Tell them how you did it. What an incredible feeling it is to help others improve their mindset and therefore their life.

Grow with the Flow

You have started to learn how to manifest everything that you want, you know to always expect nothing but the very best (and more), you know what your calling is and now you understand to wait out the storm if things get slightly bumpy when you begin to receive. You should now be attracting the right people, the right situations, and the very things to help you reach your goals and desires. Now it is time to Grow with the Flow.

When you reach this point of manifesting what you want, because things around you are reaching new levels, you will become aware that you will also have to level up mind, body, and soul. This can feel fairly daunting, and a good kinda scary at times. That is a completely natural reaction to experience when reaching new levels in your life, however, when you flow with the growth you have manifested, you will then find a comfortability within your new reality, and the daunting feeling will begin to subside. The real cheat code for levelling up your life is not always 'more effort', it is training your nervous system, mindset, and emotional maturity to handle higher levels of success without self-sabotage.

You will be exposed to new opportunities available to you because your awareness has been adapted. Take this time to always be open and accepting of new doors opening for you, because trust me, they will. Sit in every situation and simply observe, feeling a sense of flow and ease. A feeling of allowing almost.

This is a perfect time to continuously learn more about where you are and to expand your knowledge on everything that you have just manifested. Learn how to be an even better partner. Read more books on how to expand to a bigger target audience and bring in more profit from your store. Put yourself in the same rooms as the experts in your industry if you are just starting out. Observe what they do, how they do it, and take notes! Levelling up and actively growing into this new space you have created will soon become a snowball effect. It will get you prepared and ready for new levels to come. It will help you further improve and develop what you have manifested.

We can always be positively reinventing ourselves through this growth. This means making significant and deliberate changes to our lives, careers, and identities to pursue the growth, fulfillment, and alignment that we want in our lives. This does not mean fully erasing our past and forgetting the vital steps we needed to take in order for us to be here right now. Our past is so precious and important as it has made us who we are today. I know I would never change anything that I have been through. To me, it is worth its weight in gold. Every situation I have been through in the past, both good and bad, are priceless to me.

Reinventing ourselves throughout each level and stage in our lives is about embracing the new possibilities and adapting to the new circumstances. As I mentioned previously, people from our 'past lives' will look at us and think, 'You've changed', and this is where we say, 'We're supposed to'.

Something to take note of now is that as you are growing with the flow and forever evolving into an even happier and better version of You, you may become aware that what you originally thought you wanted to manifest, has now completely changed. The reason for this is more than likely because you have attracted something much better along the way. Something that you did not think was even possible previously. So, your trust in the process and the Universe has allowed you to expand your mind to what is possible for you.

The bar has been raised, and you can see that so much more is on offer.

You may have thoughts that come into your mind such as, 'I can't believe there was a time when I was so desperate for that', or 'Thank god that didn't happen because otherwise I wouldn't have this ...' When you have these thoughts and you reflect back to where you once were, you can see just how far you have come and how much you have grown. Appreciate and soak up that evolution. Life is continuously evolving and growing. Look at the planet, the technology, and the nature around us.

Once we become comfortable with the idea of our lives forever changing and accepting our personal development and growth, we really can create the life that, right in this moment, may seem impossible.

LET'S GET SPIRITUAL

Spirituality and Your Own Energy

For me, discovering, researching, and learning spirituality, to then implement into my daily life, has been hugely substantial. I personally have never followed or practiced any specific religion, mainly due to the fact that my family never raised me with any religious beliefs or had any views on religion themselves. Also, the area where I grew up was far from a religious community. Some people believe spiritualty to be connected to a form of God, and therefore believe that spirituality is religious based. As a result, they instantly discount the idea of spirituality all together, however, I personally disagree that this is the case.

Learning about spirituality and using spiritual tools that are in line with your specific needs in your day-to-day life has so many benefits. It enables you to enhance your mental wellbeing as well as your emotional and physical well-being. It gives you a stronger sense of purpose and meaning in life, which will lead to a greater sense of overall fulfilment. Spirituality helps improve our healthy coping mechanisms for when life brings us stressful challenges. Resulting in reduced feelings of anxiety and begins to form a beautiful safety net underneath us. It improves our resilience because it fosters a sense of genuine hope, trust, and optimism. All of this helps us bounce back from any adversity and challenges that we may face.

Not only does using spirituality in our day-to-day life help us with our emotions and our mental health, studies have shown that it can also improve our physical health too. Engaging in spiritual practices such as yoga and meditation can boost our immune system, due to the stimulation of production in the immune-boosting chemicals in our bodies. Reiki healing sessions literally release and remove the emotional and physical trauma trapped within our bodies. This helps us to move on from our past negativity and helps us focus on the new healthy future that we are currently working on.

Given all of the benefits that I have just listed, it is no surprise that spirituality is becoming increasingly popular. Spirituality results in less depression, less suicides, and less substance abuse. This means healthier and happier lives globally. Research has literally shown that spiritual people also tend to have a greater life expectancy. The benefits are HUGE.

I'm not saying let's all get together and start humming around the bottom of a tree (which we absolutely can!) ... but, because I have experienced personal benefits by using these tools, I want to share them with you, in hope that you can also. Whether or not you think this is for you, that is completely down to you ... but it is better to have the knowledge and not use it, than to not have the knowledge and need it, right?

Let's start with your own personal energy. Have you ever been drawn to or been mesmerised by someone who has just simply entered the room, without them even saying or doing a thing? We all have our own energy within our bodies that radiates outwards, and it surrounds us ... continuously. Many people call this our 'aura' or our 'vibe'. You know when some people just have an aura or vibe about them? Well, studies have shown that your aura/energy field is thought to extend anything from a few inches to a few feet around your whole body. This actually varies in size and shape depending on your state of mind at the time. The more you are aware of your own aura and vibe (and other peoples at that), you can begin to amend and improve it for the better.

Did you know that the electromagnetic field generated by your heart alone can be detected and measured up to several feet outside of your body? In all directions. Our energy is a constant vibration that comes from within us that permeates everything. This is heavily influenced by our values, our beliefs, and our actions. Not to mention our thoughts and feelings. As you know, everything within our own personal life, our bodies, and this world, is energy. Literally everything is always constantly buzzing, whether we physically see it or not. So, once we begin to change our internal energy using everything you are learning in this book, you will create a new energy vibration that will then radiate outward as a result.

The purpose and importance of adapting this is because you literally attract the very same energy frequencies and vibrations that you are giving out into the world. This is key information because once you are aware of this fact, you will understand that it is YOU who is in control of what you magnetize. So basically, **we need to become the energy that we want to attract.**

Some of my favorite spiritual tools which have made me see huge benefits in my energy are white sage, tarot cards, reiki healing, incense sticks, oils, yoga, meditation, and clairvoyant sessions ... we will talk about them all individually in more depth as this chapter unfolds. These are just my personal preferences, however, there are so many other spiritual tools out there available that could work for you. This is where your own ongoing research and individual preferences will definitely be more beneficial to you.

When we have completed the inside work using everything we are discussing within this book, your energy will enhance and upgrade. That is a promise. You will begin to understand and move like your vibe is a privilege to be around, because it is. People will start complimenting you on your aura and be in awe of you. This is because you have spent the precious time and effort to work on your Self for the better. Once you do this, it is also so important that you **protect and maintain it.** The work you have done, and are continuously going to do in the future, is so considerable that the results will be incredibly precious. So, you should maintain, protect, and preserve them at all costs.

Not everyone you encounter will be at your current level of self-development. This will probably create a divide and some space between yourself and others. Some people will not even be aware of the concept of 'self-development' and what work it entails ... and that is fine. You cannot force positive change on to anyone else unless they are ready and willing to receive it. As a result, it is so pivotal that you do not allow the negativity and pessimism of others to infect your energy that you have worked so hard on developing. Allow them to just be themselves. Accept them and their own personal journey as it is. Sure, you can explain your knowledge and provide the reasons why you have personally enhanced, upgraded, and bettered your life. But never force anything or get frustrated with someone who is not willing to work on themselves.

When someone comes into your life that is angry, depressed, negative, pessimistic, or critical ... offer the advice, recommend the books, but then allow them to be how they choose, and stay in your lane. Help them initially of course, give your best advice if you have been through something similar, buy them the perfect self-help book that you think they could benefit from right now, but do not let their negative vibration seep into your aura. Remind yourself of the thick glass shield we spoke about.

This 100% translates to people online too, not just the people we see face to face. Being a model who concentrates heavily on online content, I have been exposed to many situations where people online have felt the need to criticize my existence simply because I don't fit inside their box. They have disapproved of me and my life choices, verbally attacked me, have tried to have me 'cancelled', tried to degrade and devalue me, and find fault with everything about me. Luckily, my skin and aura are both thick, unbreakable, and as a result, I am very internally content. Mainly because I understand that no one who is truly confident within themselves will ever throw shade at another human. Plus, during my younger years as a stripper, standing there naked in front of strangers gives you a sense of transparency, yet confidence. The ultimate vulnerability ... but in a beautiful and empowering way.

People that feel the need to critique others online should really be questioning themselves and why they feel that others don't fit inside their box. That is their own issue and their own question to answer, not yours. If you do happen to become a victim of this behavior, it is important to understand that they are in desperate need of self-help, shadow work, and awakening. So, if anything, you should feel compassion for them that they are not growing and working towards that goal. Sadly, they clearly are not even aware of it.

The only person you have to receive validation from in this life is your Self. Least of all strangers. They do not know you as a person, so therefore their opinions are invalid. It is that simple. As long as you are forever improving, are happy and content with You and what you are doing, no negative opinions matter.

Reiki Healing and Chakras

Let's talk about reiki healing. Now this is a game changer, honestly. I am genuinely excited for you to learn, understand, and experience this. Doing your research to find a decent local healer and investing in reiki sessions is going to have insane benefits for your mind and body! I believe reiki sessions are absolutely essential if you want to be able to heal your body from your past traumas, help remove the negative blockages within your body/chakras and move forward successfully.

I was first introduced to reiki healing when I needed help with a terrible anxiety of flying. In April 2022, I was preparing myself to fly long haul from London to Las Vegas to visit Andy. Although I had flown to France, Lanzarote and Spain in recent previous years, the thought of flying was still crippling, especially long haul. I hadn't flown long haul since I was around twelve years old to Florida, so the idea of flying ten hours to Las Vegas was extremely tough.

When I was living on Worthing seafront, I was regularly visiting a beautiful family run, massage and holistic therapy salon, not that far from my home. I was visiting my therapist Lauren for weekly full body massages, Indian head massages, and reflexology massages. During one particular reflexology session, she could tell that I was feeling overwhelmed and anxious about my upcoming trip. She believed that she could potentially help to alleviate my discomfort with a few reiki healing sessions. So, she asked me to unload on to her the issues I was facing. When I explained that I was not only worrying about the safety of the flight and the plane itself, but I was also worrying about my physical health. If my lungs and heart would survive this distance that high up (I know, I know). I also had uneasy feelings because I was leaving my boy Leo for the first time. The thought of leaving my safety net of home and travelling was extremely frightening. This is when she, thankfully, introduced me to the world of reiki healing.

The simplest explanation I can offer to you on what reiki healing is and what it involves, is that it is a healing session with a trained therapist that helps unlock the blocked and negative energies within your body. All stress, anxiety and trauma from previous and current situations can be held in certain chakras within the body. Which in turn, as we well know, can cause physical, mental, and emotional distress.

Chakra (cakra in Sanskrit) means 'wheel' and refers to energy points within our bodies. These points are thought to be spinning disks of energy that should always stay open, aligned, and ideally, flowing freely. They correspond to bundles of nerves, cells, major organs, and areas of our energetic body that affect our emotional and physical wellbeing. Below, I have listed and described all seven of these Chakras for you to learn and get familiar with. What will become obvious to you is that the particular events that we have been exposed to and may have trauma with, will fester in the corresponding areas of the body. This helps us understand what we are storing in our bodies and what we need to resolve.

1. ROOT CHAKRA (Muladhara)
Governs: Stability, security, and basic survival needs.
Location: Base of the spine.

2. SACRAL CHAKRA (Svadhisthana)
Governs: Creativity, emotions, and relationships.
Location: Below the navel.

3. SOLAR PLEXUS CHAKRA (Manipura)
Governs: Confidence, self-esteem, and personal power.
Location: Upper abdomen.

4. HEART CHAKRA (Anahata)
Governs: Love, compassion, and connection.
Location: Center of the chest.

5. THROAT CHAKRA (Vishuddha)
Governs: Communication and self-expression.
Location: Throat area.

6. THIRD EYE CHAKRA (Ajna)
Governs: Intuition, insight, and clarity.
Location: Between the eyebrows.

7. CROWN CHAKRA (Sahasrara)
Governs: Spirituality and connection to higher consciousness.
Location: Top of the head.

My first experience with energy healing with Lauren was eye opening and profound. I learnt more about my physical body than I ever had done before. I realized that I was holding on to so much past trauma, emotionally and physically, which was preventing me being at ease. Only by unravelling these negativities and becoming aware of them, can we address them and finally become healed.

The trained therapist you find will lay you on a massage bed and cover you in a sheet, just like you would be if you were about to have a massage. Healing frequency music may be played in the background and specific oils and crystals may be used during the session … depending on what is needed following your initial consultation. The healer will then use healing energy transfer to unlock, remove, and heal any blockages that they may find. They will possibly ask you questions throughout your session so they can further help with the healing that you need.

You may experience heightened emotions, crying, flashbacks, visions, physical body sensations etc ... all depending on what you are there to heal and unblock. The number of sessions you will need is completely individual; however, three to four sessions will usually be recommended. Since my first session with Lauren, I completed the trip to and from Las Vegas, several times. Yes, with slight natural anxiety, however, a vast improvement had I not had the sessions with her.

Since living here, I have had two reiki sessions with a new spiritual healer that I researched and found locally. This time I was going for help coming off my beta-blocker anxiety pills. As I told you in a previous chapter, I was working on coming off the beta-blockers which, with the help of reiki healing sessions, I have now successfully achieved. I had been on the tablets for around thirteen years, so I was told by Jenny, my new healing therapist, that my heart chakra was running on overtime and did not have a calm energy at all. Once she had worked on me for the second time, I will never forget the 'healing crisis' I experienced immediately.

A healing crisis after reiki healing can be scary. Basically, it is a healing reaction, or detox reaction, normally within the first 48 hours after the session. It is luckily only a temporary worsening of symptoms. This happens when the body processes and releases negative toxins during the healing process. This may initially feel like a setback before the long-term improvement that you will experience and benefit from.

When I first experienced this, I was home alone as Andy was on tour working. My heart was erratic. It was racing, thumping, skipping beats, you name it, it was doing it! To say I was terrified was an understatement. I went to the healing session to calm my heart! I did not expect to have the complete opposite reaction! I had no knowledge on what a 'healing crisis' was, so I had no choice but to contact Jenny later that day to ask if this was normal, or if I had to go to the emergency room. Thankfully, she enlightened me on what a healing crisis was. She explained to me that because my heart chakra blockage was so intense, my heart had to find it's normal rhythm again. She advised me to do some research online, drink lots of water, avoid alcohol and caffeine, and ground myself, preferably outside.

After 48 hours of pure panic and anxiety relating to the idea that I had gone backwards on my health anxiety journey, I began to finally feel the calmness that my heart so desperately longed for. I have not been on the tablets for over a year now, and I know deep down that I will never need to go back to using them. During the 48 hours of healing after my session, Jenny also advised me to research Hridaya

Mudra, a meditation pose specifically for the heart which I will explain in more detail in this chapter.

As we know, healing our bodies and mind from past trauma and continuously learning to improve our Self is something we should always be striving for. Our personal growth is always an ongoing masterpiece which is priceless. My journey with reiki healing will also be ongoing as I know there are other areas and chakras within me that need care and healing. The idea is to remove the negative blocked energy within our bodies to then create a perfect vessel for us to live a prosperous, happy, and healthy future in.

Shadow Work

Now this is the part of the journey that many people either a, avoid doing completely or b, have not even heard of. The reason why is because, in a nutshell, shadow work can feel frightening, difficult, and as though we are going backwards. This is because you are basically bringing up and facing the unresolved demons from the past. No matter how uncomfortable it is, the benefits of doing shadow work are completely transformative. With shadow work we have to start pointing the finger at ourselves and start uncovering that we, sometimes, can be the problem. This in itself is something some people find very uncomfortable to do and will avoid doing at all costs. Let's be real, no one really likes being 'wrong' or being made to feel as though the issue lies within them. However, in order for us to live our very best lives, it is time we take the masks off. Like I mentioned before, we are our problem, and we are also our solution.

Shadow work basically involves us exploring the parts of ourselves that we may find undesirable. These can include things like negative emotions, negative impulses, and negative behaviours in which we try to repress. There is a big difference between suppressing and repressing. Suppressing parts of ourselves means that we consciously reject or prevent them. Repressing means that we are subconsciously doing so, and therefore, it means that we are not fully aware that we are even doing it.

When we begin shadow work, we will be consciously examining and integrating these repressed aspects of ourselves, rather than suppressing or denying them to come to the surface. This goes against everything our brains have been wired to do, so therefore it will feel uncomfortable. By intentionally acknowledging our shadow Self, we will be gaining a more complete understanding of ourselves and why we are how we are. In turn, this means that we can gain a clearer perspective, gain that precious personal growth and have an overall better chance at healing.

The first step is simply observing and recognising the people and situations that trigger us into experiencing strong feelings of anger, envy, guilt, anxiety, or sadness – basically any strong negative emotions. Some people find it beneficial to keep a journal and write down these particular scenarios that trigger them, so that it is easier to look back and observe similarities and patterns over time. This is when we then begin to really examine and review why this has caused us such high negative emotions. Questioning our feelings and thought processes will eventually lead us to the **real** reason why it makes us feel this way. Most likely, our subconscious mind is repeating a memory attached to those particular people and scenarios, because it feels familiar to a previous traumatic experience that we may have been exposed to.

Start observing these thoughts and feelings you experience WITHOUT JUDGEMENT. Do not shame or be ashamed of them. When you just simply observe these thoughts and feelings, without judgement, you can evaluate them from a detached view, which will therefore make it easier to dissect and most importantly, release.

Clarity comes from stillness. Pause and allow yourself to just feel whatever pain you are feeling, rather than just going down the usual path of numbing, avoiding, and running away from it. Begin to feel the feeling **fully**. Face it head on. Begin to immerse yourself in the feeling with curiosity, acceptance, care, and love. Accept that you are experiencing these feelings and be curious as to how you can work through them, and eventually, diminish them.

Practicing this each and every time that you are exposed to a situation that causes you emotional distress will help you to start understanding your shadow side, and therefore, give you an increased chance of finally healing. This also really helps encourage introspection and the understanding of our unconscious minds, patterns, and behaviours. Only then can we begin to rewrite our stories, heal emotionally, improve our relationships, and break our unhealthy habits.

If you do have an incredibly detailed and complex past, with severe trauma that causes triggers, resulting in dangerous situations, shadow work is still going to be safe and beneficial for you and your story. If working on this part of yourself alone feels too overwhelming, the best thing for you to do moving forward is to research a great therapist that specialises in shadow work. Someone to help support you, keep you accountable, and most importantly keep you safe, will be of enormous benefit.

Benefits of Hridaya Mudra/Crystals/Sage/Incense/Oils

We have discussed the transformative benefits that spirituality can have on your life, so now I am going to pass on to you my very own personal, tried and tested, spiritual tool kit. These are my favourite spiritual aids that I have implemented into my daily life to help me heal, ground myself, and evolve. By doing these simple practices and habits each day, I have improved my mental and emotional well-being, felt calmer and felt more grounded. My anxiety has massively reduced as a result of using them, and they have also been a huge help in assisting with my manifestations. As I said, there are so many more spiritual tools and practices available which you may personally prefer, so be sure to research and expand your knowledge on spirituality to uncover what will benefit you the most.

I do hope it is not the case but if you are anything like me, I find it extremely difficult to quiet my mind and meditate. I am the ultimate over-thinker, so trying to calm the voice in my head and just simply focus on my breathing is almost impossible. Anxiety provoking actually, I won't lie! As I fully understand and appreciate the potential physical and mental benefits, I tried attempting meditation for years, but to this day I am still not successful. And you know what? That's ok!

I thought there was something wrong with me specifically because I just couldn't calm the voice in my head, but yet everyone else seemed like they could, easily! Actively focusing on my breath made me feel MORE anxious. Eventually, I decided to stop trying so hard, stop beating myself up and find other avenues that could work for me. As a result, I gained more knowledge on other tools that are available which, thankfully, became equally as useful. I thought I was a lost cause when it came to meditating until my reiki healing teacher Jenny introduced me to the simple, but so effective, Hridaya Mudra meditation.

During the healing crisis that I was experiencing for the 48 hours following the heart chakra reiki session I told you about, I was calling and texting Jenny for help and advice as my heart was so erratic and irregular. Nothing was calming it down. So, she sent me a link to a blog and a 'how-to' diagram for Hridaya Mudra which is a Mudra practice specifically for the heart. As I was in such a desperate state at the time, I was open and keen to try it, regardless of my previous meditation failures. I have attached a diagram for you to see the hand pose, but the procedure and pose is this;

Sit comfortably, I prefer crossed legged in the garden or anywhere outside to really help with grounding. Place your hands with your palms facing upwards, lightly resting on your thighs or knees. Close your eyes and take some deep breaths – I personally like the 5 2 7 breathing practice but feel free to use any breathing technique that you prefer. Inhale through the nose for 5 seconds, hold for 2 seconds, and then slowly breathe out through your mouth for 7 seconds (repeat this for 2-3 minutes). You should now feel more grounded and experience an overall body relaxation. Next, take your focus to your hands. Bend your index finger and put it in the root of your thumb, like you are making a circle shape. Then place the tip of your thumb together with both the middle and ring fingers and press slightly (not hard). The little finger should be kept extended as much as possible, without any strain.

At this point you can begin to focus your mind on your specific intention, such as gratitude, healing, grounding, heart health, relaxation etc. Aim to do this for 30 minutes a day. If you can do this in one sitting, then that is great. If not, ten-minute sessions, three times a day.

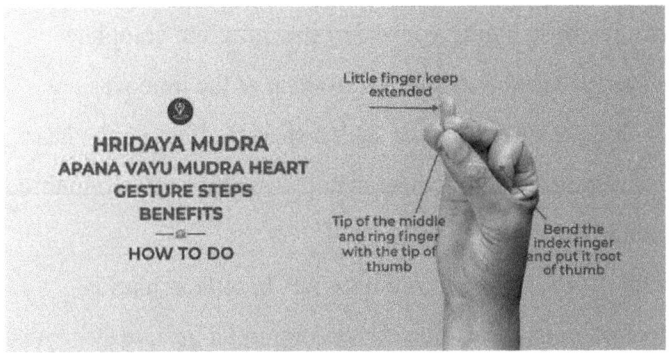

Image source – www.7pranayama.com

I did this practice for ten minutes, three times that one particular day, and the difference in my heart activity and overall anxiety was insane. I sat in the garden on the grass with the sun on my face. I put calming heart frequency music on Spotify, and I set a timer on my phone for just ten minutes to try it. My heart became calm and normal again. I felt grounded. I suddenly had a huge sense of healing. I was back in rhythm after such a long time. I even began to cry because of the relief I was experiencing. It was such a simple practice yet so, so powerful.

After I achieved the much-needed calmness in my heart, I decided to delve deeper into the benefits of this practice, and I was so surprised. What I discovered was that regular practice of Hridaya Mudra is great for your overall health and immune system, not just for your heart health. The reason being is because the practice activates the defence mechanism in the body, which helps fight against all diseases. It literally begins to cure both high and low blood pressures by bringing your heart pressure into complete alignment. What was amazing to hear at the time was not only does this Mudra have such a special effect on the heart, but it also brings immediate benefits, within just two to three seconds.

The list of benefits just continued, blood circulation increases in the heart, the circulatory and digestive system is improved, gout is improved. Stomach pain, anal diseases, acidity and heartburn, all improved! Your heart rate also either increases or slows down, depending on what is needed to normalise and stabilise your rate. It helps balance the overall energy within your heart chakra too, which as we know is associated with love, compassion, connection, and emotional wellness. So, this means that the emotional benefits are just as substantial as the physical benefits.

For me, when it comes to meditation, the simpler the better. So, this was perfect. It absolutely saved me at the time I needed it the most. Yes, this is a simple practice but do not allow the simplicity to fool you. The results are so significant. And not just if you have a blocked heart chakra.

During the practice, instead of spending the full 30 minutes focusing on my breath (which was counterproductive for me), I personally found that focusing on manifesting what I wanted to attract was so much more beneficial for me. I have used this practice many times since. When my heart has felt erratic, when I travel, or when I needed some 'grounding' time. I spend this time visualising perfect outcomes or simply visualising what I am currently grateful for in my life.

Let's now move on to crystal healing. I started using crystal energy intentionally back in 2018. However, when I look back to my childhood, I realise that I actually bought some crystals from a small witch village in Bashley, The New Forest, England. This initial exposure to crystals was when I was just ten years old. The handful of tiny crystals that I bought with my pocket money as a child were a small bundle of clear quarts and amethyst crystals, wrapped up in a small blue velvet pouch. I have kept them with me to this very day. Obviously, at the time I didn't know what they were or understand the profound benefits they were to have. I must have just been attracted to them at the time. They have all been kept in their tiny pouch to this day. On the odd occasion I do get them out to ground myself or to manifest something in particular. What I do find fascinating is that they are still extremely vibrational and energetic, even though I have never cleansed them.

That is exactly what crystals are. They are vibrational and energetic natural formations that possess metaphysical properties. They benefit and promote our physical, emotional, mental, and spiritual wellbeing ... when used in the correct way. What crystals do is they interact with the body's own energetic field to help promote healing, give protection, and enhance positive energy. There are hundreds of different types of crystals that each have their own superpowers, so I would advise treating yourself to a crystal specific book that lists all of the crystals and their individual benefits. There are specific crystals for specific needs. Some promote emotional balance and healing from past traumas, some are great manifesters and attracters, and some protect you from negativity and bad energy. They can help with boosting your self-esteem and confidence, encourage creativity and improve mental clarity and focus. Crystals are sometimes also used to balance and align the chakras, which means they are great to use during reiki healing sessions!

For me, the best way to use crystals is to hold them with a particular intention. I like to have them on me throughout the day, depending on what I need them for. You can put them in your pocket, in your bag or place them around the house. You can put them next to your bed or under your pillow to help aid sleep, or on your kitchen work top to attract positive energy and healing through the food you eat. I use them if I have an appointment that I am going to which I'm concerned or worried about … because they help with physical healing too. You can buy beautiful water bottles that are specially made to hold crystals, so you can drink their energies. Sometimes, I even shower and bath with them if I want to cleanse myself with that particular stone.

When you know what energy it is that you want to attract or remove, the best way to find out what specific crystal is for you is by holding them in your hand. You should feel visually drawn to a particular crystal in a crystal/spiritual shop and experience a physical sensation in your hand as you hold them. Many people, including myself, wear a particular crystal in jewellery to reap the benefits. Some find it substantial to meditate with them and some people place them strategically around their workspace.

Crystals absorb the energy from their surroundings, both negative and positive, so cleansing them every now and then is important to keep them pure and effective. By cleansing them, you will be removing any stagnant or unwanted energy, which as a result, will restore them and allow them to function at their fullest potential. I cleanse mine by placing them in clean fresh water in a bowl and place them in either direct sunlight or moon light. Some people also choose to cleanse them with white sage smoke or place them next to specific stones. So, feel free to research the best cleansing method that feels good and suits you.

Here I have listed just some of my personal favourites that I have known to work for me but the list available is too large to include in this book! Researching the best ones for you and your current specific needs will be hugely beneficial. Enjoy!

BLACK TOURMALINE - Black Tourmaline is a powerful grounding stone that has a deep black colour. It is believed to protect against negative energies and promotes emotional stability and grounding. This crystal is also used to cleanse and purify spaces.

PYRITE – Pyrite, also known as 'Fool's Gold', is a metallic gold stone known for its protective and grounding properties. It is often used to boost confidence, motivate, and promote mental clarity and focus. Pyrite is also believed to attract wealth and financial abundance.

CITRINE – Citrine is a vibrant yellow and white stone known for its sunny and uplifting energy. Citrine is often called the 'Merchant's Stone', associated with prosperity and success. It can also boost confidence and creativity.

QUARTS - Quartz is a versatile and powerful crystal known for its ability to amplify energy and intentions. Clear Quartz enhances mental clarity and focus, while Rose Quartz promotes love and emotional healing. Smoky Quartz is used for grounding and protection, and Rutilated Quartz enhances spiritual growth and transformation.

AMYTHEST - Amethyst has beautiful purple hues and a calming energy. It is often used to relieve stress and anxiety. It promotes a sense of tranquillity and helps aid sleeping issues. Amethyst is also believed to enhance spiritual awareness and intuition.

TIGERS EYE - Tiger's Eye is a golden-brown stone with a reflective sheen. It is known for its protective and grounding properties. It is often used to boost confidence and help motivate. It helps enhance mental clarity and focus. Tiger's Eye is also believed to attract good luck and prosperity.

BLACK OBSYDIAN – Obsidian is a black volcanic glass that offers grounding and protective properties. It is often used to shield and protect against negative energies. It helps promote emotional stability. Obsidian is also believed to support mental clarity and focus.

MALACHITE - Malachite is a vibrant green stone with swirling patterns. It boasts protective and transformative properties. Malachite helps promote emotional healing from past trauma. It supports personal growth by attracting prosperity and abundance.

JADE – Jade is typically green and is known for its association with the heart chakra. Therefore, it helps aid love and compassion. People use it to enhance emotional healing and balance. It encourages harmony and internal growth. Typically known to attract good luck and prosperity.

The next essential tool I advise you to have in your spiritual tool kit is white sage. My home, my fiancé, my dog, and myself are all covered in white sage every single time that I clean the house, or if any of us are feeling effected negatively by someone else's energy. I also make a point of blowing the sage smoke around the front, back, and garage doors to protect us and keep the home safe and secure. Burning white sage has so many benefits from air purification to the removal of negative energy that is held within the home. Not only does burning white sage have antimicrobial properties that can help kill bacteria, viruses, and fungi in the air by improving air quality, it also has many spiritual and mental benefits too.

The ritual for burning white sage around my home starts once I have finished cleaning the house fully. However, I do carry out the same ritual if there has been a certain negative situation that has arisen or if a person enters my home who is carrying a bad energy. I begin by lighting one end of the white sage bundle on my stove top in the kitchen. Once it has a substantial flame, I blow it out to create as much smoke as I can (without setting off the smoke alarms ... which I absolutely have done in the past). I use a pearl shell dish to take around with me to prevent the ash falling onto the floor, but you can use any type of plate or dish. Then, the idea is to go into all of the rooms of your home, including all of the corners, and behind the doors too. You must always do this practice with specific intentions and focus.

The sage smoke purifies and cleanses the air as well as your belongings, so setting the intention in your mind or speaking it out loud throughout this practice is essential. Throughout my ritual, I blow the white sage smoke around the house and say out loud, 'I burn this white sage to remove all of the negative energies and replace it with only positive energies. I bring about, and attract; positivity, abundance, good physical and mental health, financial freedom, confidence, loyalty, love, unexpected windfalls, celebrations and mental clarity'. When I come to white sage over the beds, I say with intention 'I remove the negativity and attract only calm, blissful sleep, tranquility and relaxation'. When I come to white sage around the front door, back door and garage I say, 'I remove all of the negative energy and attract only positive energy, keeping this house safe, secure, protected and blessed. Lastly, when I come to white sage myself, I stand in front of a full-length mirror, wafting the smoke around me, head to toe, saying with intention, 'I remove all of the negative energy, illness and blockages and I attract only positivity, good physical health, good mental health, love, success and abundance'.

Although I carry out this ritual every time I clean my home without fail, I also have had to do this with certain situations where someone's negativity has tried to seep into my aura. As we know, it is so important to protect our energy, so you may find if there is a particular issue with work, or you have had an argument with your spouse, you will want to grab the white sage and cleanse your space. As I mentioned before, you can use white sage to cleanse crystals, to help with meditating or just whenever you feel like the energy in your home is a little flat. Doing this practice with positive frequencies playing at the same time has even more power, so it might be a good idea to create a playlist specifically for this ritual.

Although using white sage is my preference, there are other alternatives available that you can burn;

LAVENDAR – Known for its calming and soothing properties. Used to help promote relaxation and tranquility.

ROSEMARY – Associated with protection and memory. Used to ward off negativity and enhance focus.

CEDAR – Known for grounding and protection. Used to purify spaces and promote stability.

THYME – Mainly used for cleaning and purifying. Used to clear stagnant energy and promote fresh starts.

YERBA SANTA – Known for its uplifting and purifying properties. Used to promote positive energy and to clear the mind.

MUGWORT – Known for cleaning, protection and altered states of consciousness. Used to offer a sense of protection, grounding, and enhances dream recall.

PALO SANTO – Known for purifying and relaxation. Helps attract positivity and enhance creativity. Used for promoting a positive mindset and mental clarity. Known to attract good fortune and reduces stress.

As you can see, they all have similar benefits so feel free to use any of these options. However, the most important thing to remember is to always use them with a particular intention. The intentional will and the energy that comes from you, combined with these plants and herbs, is where the power lies. You are cleaning away bad and stale energy to then attract and manifest abundance within your sacred place.

Yes, this process is considered more of a spiritual practice, ceremony, and devotional act that you will probably do every now and then, however, you can burn daily incense sticks too, which I also use.

Each day, I have a candle burning from when I get up in the morning until I go to bed at night. I also light my incense sticks with the candle flame. I have three incense stick holders spread out around my home and once, twice, or maybe three times a day, I will light either white sage or lavender incense sticks. These are less intense as the white sage burning rituals, but they still have great benefits.

Burning incense sticks in your home daily can offer multiple benefits which include things like; relaxation promotion, enhanced meditation and improved sleep quality. They purify the air, boost creativity, and elevate your mood. Depending on your personal taste and what scents you enjoy smelling, there are HUGE amounts of options available to you.

The possibilities are pretty much endless when it comes to incense sticks, depending on the combination of ingredients, your likes, and your intentions. Some common and most popular scents are floral, woody, spicy, resinous, and earthy notes. White sage, lavender, nag champa, fortune and positive vibes are all my personal favorites. What I would advise if you are just beginning to use incense sticks is purchasing a multipack. That way you can find out what you prefer and what benefits you and your home the most.

To me, burning white sage a few times a month and burning incense sticks daily fills both me and my home with calmness, good intentions, and a sense of unlimited possibilities.

Last but not least on my spiritual tool kit are essential oils. Essential oils are concentrated plant extracts in oil form and have so many benefits. They can be used for aromatherapy during massage sessions, on the body at night, and you can also put a few drops into your baths for you to feel their full benefits. Using oils helps us with stress relief, enhances our overall mood, and improves various physical and mental health issues.

Essential oils can help aid respiratory issues, reduce physical pains, and improve our sleep quality. Some oils are specific for general relaxation and others are used specifically for anxiety and panic attacks. Some have anti-inflammatory properties which helps with swelling and fights infections. Some help aid decongestion and therefore improve respiratory support. Some can even boost our alertness and improve focus and concentration.

My top go-to essential oils are lavender, which I spray on my pillows and bedding at nighttime (as well as a body roll on which I place on my temples, chest, wrists, and feet to help promote a decent night's sleep). A blend called 'breathe deeply' which is a blend that consists of eucalyptus, lemon, lavender, tea tree, peppermint, cardamom, and laurel leaf. I use this oil if I am feeling anxious or if I need some mental clarity. Tea tree, which I use for the antibacterial and antifungal properties when I have any skin issues or wounds. And lastly, Bergamot, which I use on my body and clothing to reduce my anxiety, lower my blood pressure when I'm feeling stressed, and to enhance my mood in general.

Oil diffusers are such a great way of releasing your chosen oils into the air. There are so many beautiful diffusers that you can buy now. Putting one in your bedroom at nighttime on a set timer to help create the perfect atmosphere to sleep is a great way of using relaxation oils. For enhancing your mood and clearing sinuses and congestion, you can put a few drops on some tissue and inhale them. If you are going to use oils on your skin, however, just make sure that they are diluted because pure oils can be a bit too harsh for our skin.

So, there you have it, my top go-to spiritual essentials that I use in my everyday life. I am in no way saying that spiritualism and the tools I have just listed above are complete cures alone. But what I am saying is that by using these alongside the other healing aids we have been discussing within this book, are all going to enhance your recovery from the past and assist you with manifesting the future you deserve.

MAKE IT YOUR NEW WAY OF LIFE

It's Your Time to Forget the Past and Create the Future You Want

As we conclude this journey together and reach the closing chapter, I have now finished sharing all of the insights and guidance that I wish I had known years ago ... with the benefit of hindsight of course. It is, however, ironic that even though I really wish I were given and understood this information years ago, to the point that it influenced the title of this book, I believe that I would not have been ready to hear or receive the advice back then.

Timing is everything. Just like the perfect timing of you finding and reading this book. The timing is so precise and significant. You were not ready in your journey to receive this message before, only now. I am a huge believer in the fact that you can give someone an opportunity, give someone the knowledge, and give someone the advice that they need to try and help them with their journey, but you cannot force them to take the action. You cannot push anyone to make a decision and actively change their own behaviors. You must have heard of the phrase, 'You can lead a horse to water, but you cannot make him drink'... that was me all those years ago when I so desperately needed this book. I know that I would have dismissed these meaningful and life-changing teachings and I would have had to experience it firsthand, struggles and all, for myself ... just as I did.

The difference between you and I, however, is that you are ready NOW. You have this book in front of you which shows that you are at the right time and the right place to receive. The right time in your life to change for the better and create the life, mind, and body that you have always wanted. It is now fully down to you to **take the action** and **be the change that you need**. Make it happen for yourself. Prove it to your Self that you are capable, and you are deserving. You do deserve this transformation, and I truly believe that you are destined for both healing and greatness.

We discussed the importance of change, the necessary healing from your past traumas, what happens in your mind when you are triggered, how important it is to remove certain things that you have in your life right now and being aware of your mind and your thoughts. We have spoken about the Law of Attraction, how to manifest and attract exactly what it is that you do want. You know how to build true confidence, and I have even armed you with a bad-ass spiritual tool kit to help you along the way.

Repetition will be your new best friend moving forward. Use repetition daily to change your autopilot, negative, subconscious mind. Do not forget that we ourselves were the ones that put the old beliefs right there in our subconscious minds from a young age, so, we also have the power to change them again as an adult. You will be able to do this only through repetition and being consciously aware of your daily thoughts and your daily actions.

Your current circumstances in your life are the direct result of your past thoughts. This is important to understand because it means that you have the capability to change it RIGHT NOW. You can put a stop to your old ways, and you can begin to heal and improve your life RIGHT NOW. You can decide to be better emotionally, mentally, and physically RIGHT NOW. The world around you and how you perceive the outside world is a direct reflection of what is inside YOU, right now. As you start to change your mindset about your past and your present life ... the world around you will only then begin to change too.

A beautiful quote I once heard by Jhené Aiko was, *'Shame on you for changing ... no, shame on you for staying the same'*. This will be something to remain conscious of moving forward. You will more than likely produce amazing and beautiful results when you implement the contents within this book into your life. This could potentially have a negative effect on the external people who are just not mentally prepared for your evolution and growth. There will be some people that you will naturally leave behind during this process, and as a result, they will then only know an old and outdated version of you. Any personal growth we may do to improve our lives sometimes will sadly not sit well with them. Let them say that you have changed. Let them feel uncomfortable with remaining in an old chapter of your life. And you know what? ... it's OK. This is something to be unapologetic for.

Another thing, by realizing a change needs to happen in your life and then actively working to heal from your past experiences, you will finally be able to **forgive and forget**. Forgive and forget the certain people who have wronged you and forgive and forget the certain situations that you have been through. We need to be **thankful** to all of the negative situations and the people who have wronged us. This allows us to finally take their power away and remove the toxic energy stored within us.

Forgetting your past negative life experiences is not only key for our emotional health and a happier future, but it is also critical to our cognitive health. Working through, healing from, and eventually forgetting the bad parts of our lives will actually help us improve the more healthy and important memories that we have stored. Subconsciously our mind, particularly during sleep, is constantly sorting out which memories to keep safe and which memories that can be removed and forgotten. Consciously, we can actively help the subconscious mind with this process of choosing what particular memories to store and what to get rid of. We have the power and the capability to forgive and forget all memories. Through conscious habits which will automatically follow through into our subconscious behaviors. The ability to forget helps us prioritise what is important to us and our future. It helps us to think better, to make better decisions, and to create a happier and healthier future.

I know there will be situations in the past that you have never had an apology for and that you will never likely receive in the future. My hope for you is that you can heal from these things that no one has ever apologised for. Forgiving these people from your past, in silence, without their knowledge, and having absolutely no intention on bringing them back into your life, is self-care. It is healing. It is self-protection and rejuvenating.

You now have all of the information, the skills and the tools that you will need to be able to forgive, and forget, the past. You can now put it all into action and start to purposefully create the future that you want.

Make Plans, Not Excuses

Henry Ford, Walt Disney, Steve Jobs, Bill Gates, Albert Einstein, Ralph Lauren, Jay Z, Daniel Ek, Ellen DeGeneres, Mark Zuckerberg, Richard Branson, Coco Chanel, Oprah Winfrey, Jessica Alba ... What do you think all of these particular people have in common?

The connecting link between all of these names is that none of them had any formal state education, yet they all became hugely successful, globally well-known, and financially abundant without. Showing you these names of just a few examples demonstrates that formal education through school, college and university is not necessarily the only path needed to achieve huge success and financial abundance.

Making internal and external life changes as well as focusing on self-help and self-development is needed to achieve sustained happiness and abundance, this we know. However, if you find yourself making excuses when you should be making plans, you will need to start honing in and finding out what the real reasons behind these excuses are.

One of the most common excuses that people make for not having the successful career and the financial security that they desire, is their belief that they do not have the right education required to obtain such things. These hugely wealthy and recognisable names show that we can achieve massive accomplishments and successes, even if we have had no formal education previously. In some cases, it is even seen as a benefit if you haven't gone through the 'tunnel-visioned' and sometimes 'capped-minded' education route, because you then are seen as a blank canvas. You are seen as adaptable, easily moulded and can be taught the required skills needed …all with no strict vision or view which can be seen as restricted.

We can gain uncapped financial abundance and career success through things like self-directed learning, entrepreneurial pursuits, and creative projects specific to what it is that we desire. The major key to remember is that career success often lies in understanding and identifying our own personal strengths, developing the relevant skills, and actively pursuing our passions. This is exactly what every single person I have just mentioned understood and used in order to attain the position that they did.

If I made the excuse of, 'I can't write a self-help book because I haven't been to university to study English literature or achieved a qualification in writing', I would have allowed that mindset to cap me and prevent the completion of this book that you are currently holding. Yes, I have had no formal education that says on paper that I should be adequate enough to write a self-help book, however, I have both the life experiences and the hindsight knowledge. As well as the passion to get my message across to the world and help the people, similar to myself, that need it. That is the essential drive and the mindset I needed to achieve this goal. You could even argue that someone who has obtained all of the 'right' qualifications may not be as relatable to yourself, as they may not have been through the similar trauma and experiences that you have.

Although this is just one common excuse that people tend to make as to why they can't do something, instead of making the necessary plans of action, there are many more excuses such as; I'm overweight, I'm not confident enough, I don't have the start-up funds, I don't live in the right country, I'm too old, I'm too young, I'm disabled. Whatever the excuse may be, it is absolutely essential that you become aware of the excuse that you are telling yourself. Notice what excuse instantly comes to your mind when you tell yourself that you are going to achieve something.

A few things you need to question when making these excuses ... why do you honestly believe that is the reason that is stopping you? Can you change it? And if you can't change it, can you change your perception and how you view it? We know now that our belief system is not always the truth, and some beliefs are just a result of our past conditioning. Once we can understand the reason as to why we are making the particular excuse that we cannot achieve something, it then gives us the opportunity to evaluate that belief and discover if there is any truth behind it.

When you start making plans towards your goals, instead of making the usual excuses, you will gain so much momentum and enthusiasm when you achieve even the smallest of results. When I started writing this book for you, for example, I knew exactly what it was that I wanted to tell you, however, I kept looking at the word count at the bottom left-hand side of my screen and thought to myself, 'There is no way that I will be able to complete an entire book'. Some days I did make the excuses, but then I finally decided to make small, realistic, and achievable plans instead. The struggle of 500 words a day eventually turned into 1300 flowing words a day. When I started to make small action plans that I could tick off, and I stopped with the excuses, I started to reach these goals. That is when the momentum built and continued to grow stronger. This is what eventually completed the book. I stopped making excuses.

The plans that you start making (and accomplishing) today are what will make you successful. Read that again. Start making the plans that will align you with your dreams and your goals. Focus on what you can do today, not on what you can't do.

A Three-Part Cocktail Mix of 'Surrendering. Habits. Gratitude'

When I say the word 'surrender' to you, how does it instantly make you feel? Many people perceive the word 'surrender' to have a weak, vulnerable, or defeatist meaning. I am here to highlight and explain to you the positive meanings of this word and the benefits it can have for you. In a philosophical, spiritual, and self-help context, surrendering signifies trusting the higher power, letting go of negative control and accepting the present moment.

By surrendering to change and surrendering to life, it does not mean that you simply sit back and watch life happen to you, like a victim. It means that, of course, you can still apply aligned action, have constructive thoughts, and set out specific goals to reach … it just means that you will be flowing with life instead of going against everything that happens to you. By surrendering you will gain feelings of trust, peace, and lightness. You release the internal negative emotions and the self-inflicted negative expectations that you have. You will become adaptable and at ease even though you are actively striving to achieve your important life goals.

Surrendering is about accepting rather than forcing things to be a certain way. By accepting and surrendering you reduce stress, anxiety, and worry. When you take action and make constructive steps to move forward from the place of surrendering, it is of the highest and purest quality. This is because it is of an unbiased, trusting, and relaxed mindset.

Once you have finished this book, positive changes and healing will begin to happen, therefore, you will be exposed to new opportunities which will in turn, level you up. That is when you will have to allow yourself to surrender to all which is about to come your way. Surrendering **is not** a sign of weakness. It is a sign of strength and courage that you can trust in something higher than your own mind. Trusting, surrendering, and allowing the process to happen is so powerful, it will make you resilient.

When you surrender to the Universe and allow for this self-development, you will notice that your conscious daily habits will change. The new daily habits that you create today will be what changes your life tomorrow. Even the smallest of habits that you may initially believe are insignificant. Initially changing our daily habits, no matter how unimportant we may think they are, will take conscious effort as our brains are wired to resist the change.

So, start small and focus on changing one negative habit at a time. This allows your brain to adjust and then build the momentum that it needs. Start by being specific about the goal at hand. Then set the goal to be completed within a certain time frame that you can realistically achieve. By doing this, you are more than likely to have success and see the results that you desire. Always, always celebrate even the smallest of wins when it comes to changing your daily old habitual patterns. These successes are what shapes your future Self!

Lastly, in this Surrender. Habit. Gratitude cocktail is the much-needed gratitude ingredient. I have a tattoo of old English scrip from the top to the bottom of my left shin that reads, 'Whoever has, will be given more, and he will have an abundance. Whoever does not have, even what he has, will be taken from him'. This essentially means that those who have gratitude and are receptive to and utilize gifts and opportunities in life, will be given more and will eventually have an abundance of all. While those who are not grateful, not receptive to opportunities and gifts, even what they have, will be taken from them.

The more gratitude you have in life, the more things you will attract to be grateful for in the future. If you are not grateful for anything you currently have in your life, the more you will lose because you just simply do not appreciate them, no matter how small or basic.

Gratefulness is a major factor in manifesting and attracting more abundance, so, the more you can start being grateful for today, the easier it will be to manifest more of the same. I know that some days it will be really difficult to see the positives and see the things in your life to be grateful for, but trust me, they are always there. Even if it is as simple as having the spare time to read this book right now. You might have to dig deeper some days but even on our worst days, there are always things to be thankful for.

Maybe one of your new daily habits could be to bring your awareness to what you are currently grateful for. You don't need to write them down each day, however, when you go to bed each night, reflect on the positive things that happened throughout your day and what you are thankful for. By doing this, you start changing your mindset to focus on a more positive outlook. You then change your internal energy and vibration ... which as we know, will attract more of the same.

You also start to recognise the things that you may have taken for granted previously. You will notice that the list each night will become longer. Savour the positives and dwell on them each night before bed and you will become a magnet for manifesting, even when you are sleeping!

There Is Only the Eternal Now

The final, critical discussion that we need to have together is about the understanding and the realisation that there is only ever the present moment, and the forever eternal now. What I mean by this is that the present moment is the only real reality, and it is all we ever have. This means that both the past and the future are mental concepts only. The past lives only in our memory which is stored in the brain, and the future is an anticipation and a vision, again, only a concept made within our minds. True living and true experience exist only when you are being fully present and fully aware in the moment, now. By fully focusing and embracing in the present moment and the eternal now, you transcend the illusion of time, and therefore of all the anxieties that are associated with both the past and the future.

The way to be in the eternal now and be in the present moment, fully, is simply by becoming aware of the now. Bring your awareness to the NOW. Try this, be aware of your physical body in the room that you are currently in, in this very moment, right now. Become aware of your mind and your thoughts as they become aware of this 'now'. Bring your awareness to the space that your physical body is taking up within the area that you are currently in. Bring your awareness to the vibrating energy within your being. That is awareness and that is being fully immersed in the eternal now.

The human mind will always try and attempt to over-think this process and make you believe that you have to dissect and mentally understand HOW to live in the eternal now. When in fact, the very opposite is true. Unfortunately, the egotistic mind will never completely understand this. Being fully aware of the present eternal now is a place that is completely free from the logical thinking mind.

By bringing your awareness, physically and mentally, to the eternal now and the present moment, you start to unlock a lot of valuable benefits. You unlock complete presence that is free from pain and unhappiness. You gain the understanding of timelessness, and you can begin to achieve your infinite blissful potential, in this moment. You can fully experience pure life, without the negatives of holding on to the past or worrying about the future. This sweet spot is a complete timeless state where infinite possibilities really do exist. You can be the intentional creator of your life in the present moment, without being held back by pain from the past or anxiety about the future.

By me describing the eternal now concept and by explaining how bringing your awareness to the present moment, I hope you caught even a glimpse of this for yourself, even for a second. As human beings, trying to remain in the eternal now and be in the present moment is difficult, however, even if you can witness this even for only a split second, it shows that you are capable of being there. So, try not to be too harsh on yourself if you struggle being here for longer than a few seconds. By practicing this on a regular basis, that moment will eventually begin to get stronger, and you will be able to hold on to it for a longer length of time. It is similar to a muscle that you need to work on in order to build its strength.

Spiritual enlightenment is a result of being fully aware and being in the eternal now, most of the time. No pain from the past and no anxiety about the uncertainty of the future can reach you within the now. The book, 'The Power of Now', written by Eckart Tolle is an incredible book solely dedicated to this subject. This book will help you to delve deeper into the understandings of the present moment, and the true power of living in the now.

In the meantime, moving forward, every time you may feel as though you are struggling with anything that we have discussed within this book, bring your awareness back to the eternal now, so you can find peace and clarity within the present moment.

An Ongoing Masterpiece

You will know by now, as we reach the summary of this book, that the 'work' advised in these pages will take time, determination, care, and patience. Unfortunately, there is not just one particular action or one simple conscious thought that is an 'instant fix' for our journey in life. Nor is there a specific time frame for achieving any of these goals. Every person is different. Every person has been through their own personal traumas and therefore has a vastly different recovery timescale. Every person has a different view on what success is to them and has a different life purpose and calling.

As you work through, re-read these pages, and implement each area into your own life, my hope for you is that you can begin to enjoy the process and the journey as it unfolds ... not just remaining unhappy and unfulfilled, focusing only on the destination and the end result. Many people oversee just how beautiful the 'now' and the 'journey' are, and they sadly become fixated only on the end results. How many times have you heard someone say, or you have even said yourself, 'I will be happy only when ...'? By telling yourself that you will only be happy 'when' you have achieved something or 'when' you have manifested that object or thing, you are not appreciating or being grateful for the now. By having that mindset, you are not living in the now. You are not consciously being aware. What happens then is you will miss out on all of the beautiful things around you to be grateful for.

Sure, you may not have everything that you want right now, or you may not be the way you want to be right now, but even the idea of changing and 'working on it' is enough to be grateful for. It is a process. Many people, like I mentioned before, sadly do not even reach that level of awareness, let alone actually do something about evolving.

The fact that you are actively striving to achieve greatness and striving for a better way of life is enough to be happy and positive for right now. All the while you are growing, you are evolving, which is simply beautiful in itself.

Every single person on this planet, currently existing and previous, no matter how advance they are in their industry and profession, are always forever learning. No one is a complete master at life itself, no matter what level they are at. Start to savour your own journey. Appreciate the steps that you are making and the growth that you are achieving, daily. Relish in the experiences that you have. Find the joy in the doing. Remember that the 'problems' we are faced with are not meant to be 'stop' signs as such, they are in fact guidelines. Surrender and allow them to signpost you throughout your life. See them as blessings in disguise.

Everything that you have learnt here is something that you can start using today and you can continuously use until your very last breath. The life you will be experiencing in 1,2,3 or more years from right now is solely based on the decisions and daily habits that you start doing today.

Your life is an ongoing masterpiece that should never be ignored, slept on, or underestimated. Your life is a blank canvas, so, begin to paint it with purpose. Every single day of your life is an opportunity to grow, heal, learn, and manifest. Every single day of your life is a special occasion so always get up and show up. You did not wake up today to be mediocre. Dress well, make the effort, look the best you can look at all times. Wear your favourite outfit, put on your best lingerie, look and feel beautiful/well-dressed/smart. By doing this, you set your mind up to be fully present, and you begin to live your life with purpose. It shows that you take your life seriously and that you appreciate being alive ... because we should! The sobering fact is that we are here for only a short period of time so why not make it the absolute very best that we can make it?

When you have days that you need a reminder of what strength looks like, look inward at your Self. Look at everything that you have been through and achieved to date. Look at everything you have managed to move past and overcome. You are the strength that you need. You are a living, breathing reminder that you have the strength needed to hold on and carry on. You have survived every single one of your worst days.

When searching 'How long does it take to create a masterpiece' on Google, the result is – 'The time it takes to create a masterpiece varies greatly depending on the field, the complexity of the work, and the artist's experience and dedication, but it generally requires sustained effort and dedication over an extended period of time'.

You think it takes 'time', but it actually takes 'alignment'.
May the rest of your life, be the best of your life'

AFTERWORD

People that meet me now meet and see only the positive, outgoing, and optimistic version of myself that I have worked so hard to achieve and maintain. They meet the strong-minded survivor that I am today, which was only the result of the growth and on-going hard work that I have been committed to, and continued to put in. If I do however, for whatever reason, happen to explain my factual past life experiences, and my life story so far, they find it very hard to comprehend or believe. Explaining my past trauma, past realities, and the overall previous person that I once used to be, they are taken back and very shocked that I could have developed into the person that I am today.

Now I see life, my Self, other people, and all experiences in a whole different light to what I did years ago. That is all down to discovering everything that we have just discussed within these pages. I want that for you. I want you to evolve and heal from your past. I want you to change how you feel about your current situation in life and the enormous potential of your future, for the better. I want people on the outside looking in to be proud of you and your self-development. I want you and other people to be in awe of your success, and to recognise just how far you have come from your traumatic experiences and difficult past. That is exactly the reason why I wrote this book and manifested it to reach you right now.

My childhood was difficult, some of my very first memories as a child are of my parents arguing, guns, drugs, divorce, and sexual abuse. My teen memories are filled with a toxic relationship which broke my soul and made me question trust in all human interactions. My early twenties memories are filled with the start of a thirteen-year health and travel anxiety journey, sleeping with men to survive, detachment from family and feeling as though I would always be in a downward spiral of depression.

It was not until I was around twenty-eight that I was actually able to understand and begin to implement the Law of Attraction, begin to face and heal from my past traumas and start to rewire my brain for the better. Since then, my life has dramatically changed for the better and I can honestly say that with this knowledge I know now, I will never hit that rock bottom again.

From child abuse, toxic relationships, stripping, being broke, being stalked and a head injury that resulted in chronic anxiety that was absolutely crippling, I managed to pull myself out of that reality and mindset and eventually gained a happy, optimistic, and grateful attitude. So, believe me when I say, if I can use what we have discussed in this book to gain true happiness and an improved life, then you really can too. Anything is possible, but only if you **want** the change and you make a promise to yourself that you will do it.

In the earlier chapter, GET RID OF WHAT YOU DON'T WANT – 'How to deal with roadblocks', I shared a story with you about my encounter with a stalker who harassed me for seven years. Since the duration of writing this book for you, there has been a significant development which I believe is important to finalise and share with you.

I was contacted by the police in February 2025 explaining that the stalker was finally being charged with breaching the restraining order and that he was due to present his plea in two separate hearings. In March I was contacted again explaining that on both hearings, he had pleaded 'Not Guilty'. They told me that as a result of him pleading not guilty, the case will be due to go to Crown Court within the next few months, so all I had to do was prepare myself for appearing in court via a video call. Amazing, I thought. After seven years of pain, abuse, feeling trapped, scared, and let down by the justice system, all I had to do now was to wait for the upcoming court date confirmation and it will all finally be over … not long now and I will finally be free to live my life.

When I came to writing the final chapter of this book, I received an email from the police. But not the email that I had longed for. I was expecting the email from the police officer to be a confirmation of the date and time for the court date, however, that was not the case. The police officer began to write 'Good morning Sam, there has been a significant development which I am required to inform you about. The defendant in the case is deceased ...' He had taken his own life.

The sudden surge of mixed emotions filled my entire body. Shock, frustration, anger, sadness, guilt, injustice, disbelief, anxiety, and relief. Although this person put me through seven years of hell, anxiety, and abuse ... no one deserves to die, and I would never wish that on anyone.

I longed for this chapter of my life to be over, but this was far from the outcome that I had so desperately needed. Frustrated that I had informed the police of the suicide note that he had written a year and 5 months prior to this happening. Angry that no one had safeguarded him and given him the help that he clearly so desperately needed. Sadness at the fact that both him and I had been let down (in different ways) by the police throughout all of this. A feeling of guilt because although I know, and understand, that I was not responsible for his death, his obsession and fixation with me was the reason why he ended his own life. A sense of relief that he could no longer harm me or ruin my life anymore. It was all now finally over. The feeling was, and still is, completely surreal.

The reason why I have added the case conclusion in the afterword for you is because although my intention for writing this book is for me to be able to help and assist you with your past and your journey, I have realised that I am also continuing to help and heal myself. What I noticed and came to the realisation of is that when I came to the end of writing this book, the chapter with the stalker also came to an end. Just as my Reiki healing teacher Jenny explained to me that there was a reason for my writer's block. This again, is proof that timing is everything.

Right now, I am not sure if having gone through this trauma with the stalker is something that I will ever 'get over', but by continuously implementing everything I have just shared with you in these pages, I know it will give me a considerable chance of healing and an ability to move forward.

You can never break a person who finds beauty in everything, even in the pain. They turn scars into wisdom, struggles into strength and setbacks into comebacks.

I have always said that if I can reach and help at least one person by writing this book then all of the pain and trauma that I have endured in my life will be completely worth going through. I understood internally that one day I would be in the position to tell the story of how I overcame what I have been through, and it will be someone else's survival guide.

I know I was built this strong for a purpose and that purpose is you. And for that I thank you. I was put on this Earth to make a positive difference. For you.

This is my calling, and I promise to you that I will deliver.

BOOK NOTES:

BOOK NOTES:

BOOK NOTES:

BOOK NOTES:

How to get in touch with me

Instagram:

@whatiwishiknewyearsago

Facebook:

@whatiwishiknewyearsago

Website:

www.whatiwishiknewyearsago.com

Email:

whatiwishiknewyearsago@outlook.com

Please feel free to share your stories and images with this book to be featured

www.ingramcontent.com/pod-product-compliance
Lightning Source LLC
Chambersburg PA
CBHW050110170426
43198CB00014B/2526